ISBN 0 361 06093 9
Copyright © 1984 Purnell Publishers Limited
Published 1984 by Purnell Books, Paulton,
Bristol BS18 5LQ, a member of the BPCC group.
Phototypeset by Quadraset Limited
Printed and bound in Italy by
Poligrafici Calderara s.p.a. Bologna

Performance Cars

The Publishers would like to express their thanks to the following for their valuable help in compiling this book: BL Heritage, Mr Michael Worthington-Williams of Sotheby's, Motor Vehicles Manufacturers' Association—USA, Detroit Public Library Automotive Collection, Kodak Museum, Veteran Car Club of Great Britain, National Motor Museum, Christie's South Kensington Ltd, Mr Peter Hull and the Vintage Sports Car Club, Mr C. M. Booth's Motor Museum at Rolvenden—Kent, *Autocar*, Musée de L'Automobile Francaise—St. Dizier, Stephen Langton Ltd. Special gratitude to Mr Stewart Skilbeck of Selby, Mr Robert Laycock of Malton, Mr Ken Barley of Boroughbridge, Mr John Bentley of Batley and Mr Jim Clark of Selby, Yorkshire for allowing their own veteran or vintage cars to be photographed for this book. Special thanks to Mr Tony Davis for his extensive editorial help.

Written by **Peter Roberts**
Photos supplied by **Peter Roberts**
Edited by **Moira Butterfield**
Designed by **Sarah Williams**

Contents

Introduction

Performance cars are cars with above-average performance . . . not simply faster, but cars that handle well, with roadholding, steering and braking to match their speed and acceleration. Racing cars are the ultimate in performance cars, for all other considerations are subordinated to outrunning rivals. Among road-going cars the superb and expensive machines of Lamborghini, Ferrari, Maserati, Aston Martin and Porsche are obvious examples of performance cars, but a car need not have a big, sophisticated engine to qualify for the term. The little Mini-Cooper S, a competition version of the ordinary Mini, outperformed everything in its class in its day, as its string of rally victories proved. The four-wheel-drive Range Rover, now standard equipment for expeditions to the wild places of the earth, is an outstanding performer over terrain that would stop most vehicles. The essential thing is that a car should be above average in its class. Standards grow higher, of course. They have risen steadily over the first century of motoring and continue to rise, today's mundane family saloon being a better performer than the sports model of yesteryear, though that was coveted in its day. This book includes performance cars of all ages and classes since Karl Benz drove the first 100 years ago. Some of the cars pictured were designed to break records, others to provide comfortable touring, but all were, or are, performers of their time.

The Experimental Years 1885–1900

The first horseless carriages were steam-driven and were virtually buses — large vehicles carrying fare-paying passengers rather than personal transport. They developed in the England of the 1820s, running over newly built roads to link towns, but they were unpopular with horse owners and were subjected to extortionate tolls and later to stringent speed limits (2 mph in towns, 4 mph in the country). The growth of railways — also steam-powered — soon put them out of business but by then inventors were experimenting with gas and petrol engines and in 1885 two Germans, working independently and unknown to each other, made the breakthrough that led to motoring as we know it. It thrived particularly in France where, within a remarkably short time, cars were being raced to show off their performance.

Benz 1885

This three-wheeler was unarguably the best performer of its day because it had no competition; it was the world's first car that really worked. Built by Karl Benz, at Mannheim in Germany in 1885, it had a water-cooled single-cylinder ¾ hp petrol engine turning at up to 400 rpm. A large, horizontal flywheel also served as the starter, and power was transmitted to the back axle by chains. On his first drive Benz hit a wall and later the car had often to be dragged back by horses, but eventually he had it running fair distances; "I may have reached 10 mph," he wrote. However, police restricted him to 4 mph in town and 7 mph in the country.

Daimler 1886

At Canstatt, only 60 miles from where Benz worked in Mannheim, motoring's other great father figure, Gottlieb Daimler, was engaged on similar work, though curiously they never met. Daimler's air-cooled engine turned twice as fast and set the standards for all subsequent petrol engines, but while Benz was making his car in 1885, Daimler put his engine in a motorcycle and a motor-boat, and it was a year later before he put one into a cart and created his first car, which could carry four at 10 mph.

Certainly the prettiest of early cars, this *vis à vis* with a two-cylinder Daimler engine of 15 hp was made by the French ironmongery firm of Peugeot, who branched into bicycle manufacture in 1885 and made a steam car in 1899, but then adopted Daimler engines. For a publicity stunt in 1892 Peugeot had a car like this follow a cycle race from Paris to Brest and back, a distance of 1,272 miles, and though not as fast as the cyclists themselves finished the journey at an average speed of 10 mph, as a result of which Peugeot sales that year totalled 29 cars, compared with only five in 1891.

Peugeot 1892

Canstatt-Daimler

By 1899 Daimler's company was producing not only cars, but a car specially for racing. This pioneering speedster, based on his Phoenix tourer, had a four-cylinder 5.5 litre engine giving a top speed of about 50 mph, but it had a short wheelbase and a high centre of gravity which made it unstable. It was not a success and production ceased in 1900 after Wilhelm Bauer was killed at the wheel of one when it ran wide on a hill climb and crashed. The importance of the car was that after Daimler had modified it to become longer, lower and more powerful, it became the first Mercedes, forerunner of a long line of high-performance cars.

Peugeot 1894

The scene is before the start of the world's first motoring contest — a timed reliability trial in 1894 over the 80 miles between Paris and Rouen. Twenty-one cars — some petrol-engined and some steam-powered — set off at intervals and the £200 first prize was eventually shared between a Panhard-Levassor and this rear-engined Peugeot, one of five similar cars in the competition, which averaged a speed of around 12 mph. The engine was a Daimler V-twin 1 litre of 12 hp. An optional extra offered by Peugot at this time was a whip with which to beat off the dogs that harried pioneer automobilists.

The world's first motor race took place in the next year, 1895, from Paris to Bordeaux and back, a distance of 732 miles. Fifteen petrol-engined cars, six steamers and an electric competed, the winner being Emile Levassor, partner with Louis-Rene Panhard in a firm which had built its first car four years earlier, with a front-mounted engine driving the rear wheels in what was to become the conventional layout. Levassor should have handed over to another driver on the way to Bordeaux but was so early the man was sleeping, so Levassor carried on all the way, arriving in Paris six hours ahead of his nearest rival.

Panhard-Levassor 1895

Knight

The first British petrol-engined car was built in Surrey in 1895 by John Henry Knight, who had previously made steam cars. It had a single-cylinder, water-cooled engine and was capable of about 9 mph. Knight made only the one car, in which he was possibly short-sighted, because in 1896 the speed limit was lifted to 12 mph and the need for a man to walk in front of the car was abolished. However, the first cars on the roads of Britain were all from the continent.

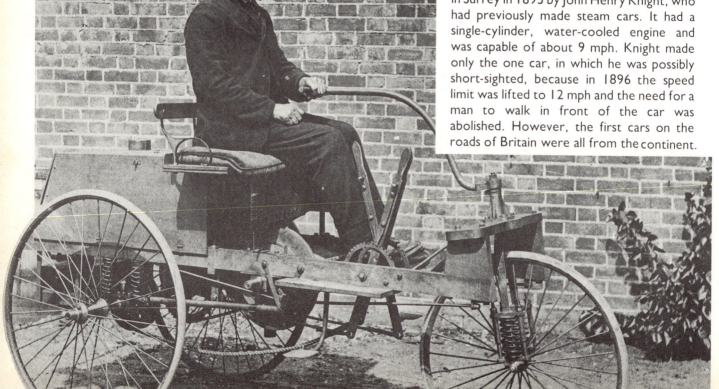

La Jamais Contente

The first world land speed record was established by a Frenchman, the Comte Gaston de Chasseloup-Laubat in 1898 when he drove a Jeantaud electric car at 39.24 mph over a measured kilometre near Paris and proclaimed himself the fastest man on earth. Camille Jenatzy, a Belgian nicknamed the Red Devil because of his red hair and beard, accepted the implicit challenge and took this electric car of his own design, *La Jamais Contente* (Never Satisfied) to the same road and reached 42.42 mph. A duel between the two men followed in which the record shifted four times within five months, eventually remaining with Jenatzy at 65.79 mph, the fastest record ever credited to an electric car.

Camille Jenatzy

Panhard-Levassor 1899

By 1899 inter-city races were well established on the continent and motor racing's first ace was Panhard pilot Fernand Charron, a former racing cyclist (like many early motor racers) who had won the Marseilles–Nice and Paris–Amsterdam events of 1898. In 1899 the main race was from Paris to Bordeaux, 353 miles, which he covered in 11 hours 43 minutes at an average of 33 mph in this four-cylinder 3.3 litre 12 hp car with distinctive cooling pipes in front of the bonnet. Charron was followed home by two more Panhards. After his victory, he was offered £2,000 for the car. He declined it.

Veteran Performers 1901–1906

Progress from the first crude carts with engines bolted on, to viable, recognisable cars was phenomenally swift. Electric ignition replaced hot tubes; honeycomb radiators replaced cooling tubes; steering wheels replaced tillers and pneumatic tyres were introduced. There were more than 200 different car makes (half of them American) in 1900, and 700 by 1905. There were steam cars, quiet and powerful but needing much attention on the road, and electric cars, limited by their batteries to running at a reasonable speed for a short distance or for a reasonable range at low speed. The petrol engine won through. The competitive nature of man and the excitement of speed meant that racing grew, with engines becoming ever bigger and bodies growing lighter mainly because of holes bored everywhere possible!

Mercedes 1902

Gottlieb Daimler built the first Mercedes in 1901 at the behest of Emil Jellinek, one of his sales agents in France who, after racing the Canstatt-Daimler without great success, got him to make it longer and lower. He also persuaded Daimler that the cars would sell better in France with a less obviously German name. Mercedes was, in fact, the name of Jellinek's daughter. The new car was an instant winner, achieving 53 mph in races. The 1902 version pictured was a tourer with a four-cylinder 5.3 litre engine of 28 hp and a speed of 36 mph, but the same chassis also accommodated limousine and racing bodies with engines which within a couple of years had reached nearly 12 litres in size.

Serpollet Steamer

At this time there was still a battle for supremacy between petrol and steam engines — and, to a lesser extent, electric power. Leon Serpollet was a French pioneer of steam. His first cars burned coke; but in 1900, when this car was built, he began using paraffin burners to heat the steam generator, which was beneath the rear seats and close to the under-floor engine of four cylinders and 956 cc. He was backed financially from this time by an American, Frank Gardner, and in 1902 at Nice, in a bigger-engined steamer, Serpollet took the world land speed record to 75.06 mph. But when he died in 1907 his firm died with him.

Locomobile Steamer

Steam was particularly popular in the United States and, of eight thousand cars on American roads in 1901, four thousand were Locomobile steamers. The firm's four-storey factory at Bridgeport, Connecticut, where 20 cars a day were produced, was the world's biggest.

The Locomobile had a 14-inch boiler under the driver's seat, powering a twin-cylinder engine, the main snag about the tiller-steered car being that it was excessively thirsty and needed more water every 20 miles or so. In 1903 Locomobile abandoned steam for petrol engines.

Stanley Steamer

The name of Stanley was the longest-lived in steam. Twins E. E. and E. O. Stanley built their first car in 1897 and they continued to be made until 1927. The picture shows George Eastman of the Kodak photographic concern riding with a friend in a 5.5 hp Stanley tourer of 1902, which was the same year Stanley began entering races. Within a few years there were streamlined racers running under such names as Wogglebug, Teakettle and Rocket, and in 1906 a steamer driven by Fred Marriott achieved 127.66 mph at Daytona Beach in Florida, though this was never recognised officially as a record. The driver of a Stanley was confronted by a daunting area of dials and gauges, but many of the cars were used by American police and fire departments.

White Steamer

The steamers made in Cleveland, Ohio, by Rollin White — originally a sewing machine manufacturer — had a more viable range; they could travel up to 100 miles without needing more water, and production was around a thousand a year when this model was built in 1905. In the same year Walter White drove a 40 hp steamer in America's Vanderbilt Cup race, which had to be abandoned because the crowd got out of control. Another racing version, Webb Jay's Whistling Billy, covered a mile at 74.07 mph in 1905 and eventually achieved a top speed of over 90 mph. President Theodore Roosevelt had a White at the White House, which helped to make it the most famous name in steam after the Stanley.

Mors 1901

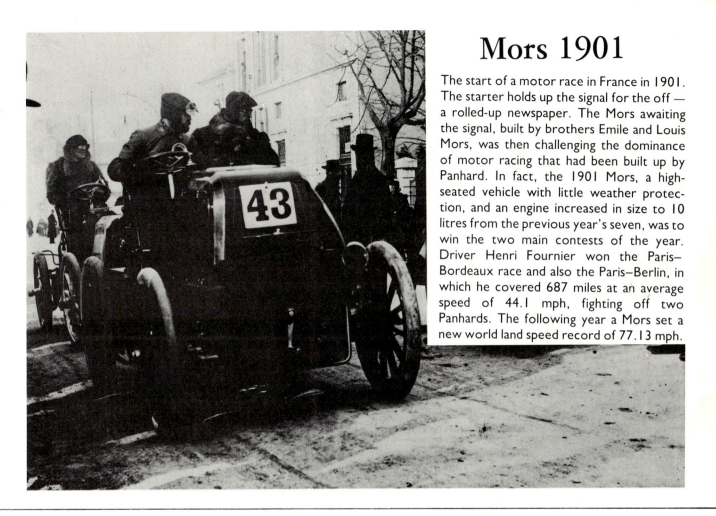

The start of a motor race in France in 1901. The starter holds up the signal for the off — a rolled-up newspaper. The Mors awaiting the signal, built by brothers Emile and Louis Mors, was then challenging the dominance of motor racing that had been built up by Panhard. In fact, the 1901 Mors, a high-seated vehicle with little weather protection, and an engine increased in size to 10 litres from the previous year's seven, was to win the two main contests of the year. Driver Henri Fournier won the Paris–Bordeaux race and also the Paris–Berlin, in which he covered 687 miles at an average speed of 44.1 mph, fighting off two Panhards. The following year a Mors set a new world land speed record of 77.13 mph.

Oldsmobile Curved Dash

The Oldsmobile was America's best-selling small car with 6,500 made when Ransome Eli Olds sent two of his products of early mass production lines on a publicity stunt in 1905. It was a transcontinental race over 4,400 miles of poor, sometimes treacherous, roads from New York to Portland, Oregon. The cars were known as Curved Dash Oldsmobiles because of the shape of the body in front of the riders' legs. They had single-cylinder 1.5 litre 5 hp engines under the seats, two gears and a speed of around 20 mph for a petrol consumption of around 20–30 mpg. This figure was important because petrol became dearer and harder to get as the cars went West. Old Scout, the winner, arrived in 44 days.

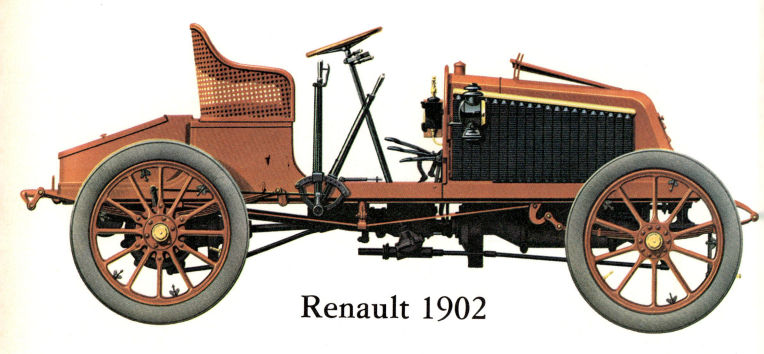

Renault 1902

The Paris–Vienna Race of 1902 was the most ambitious of the intercity series and hailed as 'the Race of Races'. The overall winner of the race, and also of the light car class, was a 16 hp four-cylinder Renault of a mere 3.8 litres. Marcel Renault, who with his brothers Louis and Fernand had founded the firm in 1898, drove it across the finishing line 35 minutes ahead of the next arrival.

This did not stop engines becoming bigger but it showed that engine size was not all-important. This was the first year that Renault had made their own engines. Previously they had bought in from other manufacturers. A remarkable feature of the Renault was that it had always employed shaft drive, rather than a chain or belt, from the start of the company.

Panhard 1902

This tile commemorates Panhard's performance in the Paris–Vienna race. The racing spanned 615 miles, including Austria's Arlberg Pass, where the cars were required to climb 5,000 ft. in ten miles, with the unfenced road ending on one side in a precipitous drop. Only 80 out of some 130 entrants completed the course. Panhard cars had become still bigger and Henri Farman, who won the big car class at an average speed of 38.7 mph, was driving a 70 hp 13.7 litre.

De Dietrich 1903

The French firm of De Dietrich, which had factories in Alsace and Lorraine, entered seven 45 hp cars of 9.9 litres and three 30 hp cars of 5.7 litres for the big race of 1903 — from Paris to Madrid. English driver Charles Jarrott was in third position, in one of the big cars, when the race was stopped after 342 miles at Bordeaux because of the number of fatal accidents. One who died was a De Dietrich driver; another was Marcel Renault. The cars were impounded and shipped back to Paris by train; 'the Race of Death' was the end of inter-city racing. One of the smaller De Dietrichs was driven by Camille du Gast, the only woman competitor, who was lying sixth until she stopped to give first-aid to a team-mate who crashed after hitting a dog.

Napier 1902

Racing driver Charles Jarrott has the wheel; Montague Napier rides as passenger on a run from London to Oxford in one of the two-seaters Napier built for the new-style carriage trade of 1902. This had a four-cylinder 12 hp engine; two years later Napier was to become celebrated for introducing the first successful six-cylinder engine, after which the company concentrated on six-cylinder models. They were race-bred. Napier had begun making cars in 1900 after carrying out modifications to a Panhard (such as converting its tiller steering to wheel steering) on behalf of Selwyn Edge, another pioneer racing driver, who won the 1902 Gordon Bennett race from Paris to Innsbruck (run as part of the Paris–Vienna race) at the wheel of a Napier.

Wolseley 1902

Wolseley's car production began in Birmingham in 1899 with Herbert Austin (later Lord Austin) as manager, and by 1902, when 500 cars had been sold and this advertisement appeared, it was Britain's leading car company. In that year it introduced a four-cylinder 5.2 litre car capable of 52 mph; it also had a single-cylinder 5 hp car and a twin-cylinder 10 hp of 2.6 litres in its catalogue. As the ad suggests, the Wolseley company made a feature of performance and it was one of the first British competition cars, used firstly in trials and from 1902 in racing. Thirty hp Wolseleys with four-cylinder 6.4 litre engines, and 45 hp cars with three-cylinder 8.2 litre engines, took part that year in the Paris–Vienna races; they also appeared in the 1903 Paris–Madrid when a Wolseley riding mechanic was one of the fatalities.

THE WOLSELEY

FOR RELIABILITY SPEED AND ELEGANCE.

THE WOLSELEY TOOL & MOTOR CAR CO LTD

ADDERLEY PARK. BIRMINGHAM.

Royce 1904

This was a Rolls-less Royce, the first car built by Henry (later Sir Henry) Royce, seen at the wheel with the Duke of Connaught as his passenger. When he made it he had yet to meet the Hon. Charles Rolls. Royce was an impoverished engineer making cranes in Manchester until friends started bringing him cars to repair. He looked at them, said: "I can do better than this," and built the two-cylinder 1.8 litre car pictured. (The apprentice about to crank it into life later became Lord Brabazon of Tara.) There was nothing revolutionary about the car but it worked well and was exceptionally quiet. An acquaintance enthused about it to Charles Rolls.

Rolls-Royce 1906

The Hon. Charles Rolls, wealthy racing motorist and car salesman, became Royce's partner and this was their first model, a six-cylinder 20 hp car, seen re-starting on a one in six gradient with nine up in Sydenham in 1906. To win publicity for the new firm Rolls drove one in the 1906 Isle of Man TT race and finished the 161 mile race 27 minutes ahead of the opposition, a Berliet, a Darracq, a Clement and a Beeston-Humber. His average speed was 39.43 mph. This success brought Royce more orders than he could meet and the company bought land at Derby to build bigger premises. There they decided to build only one model — the best in the world.

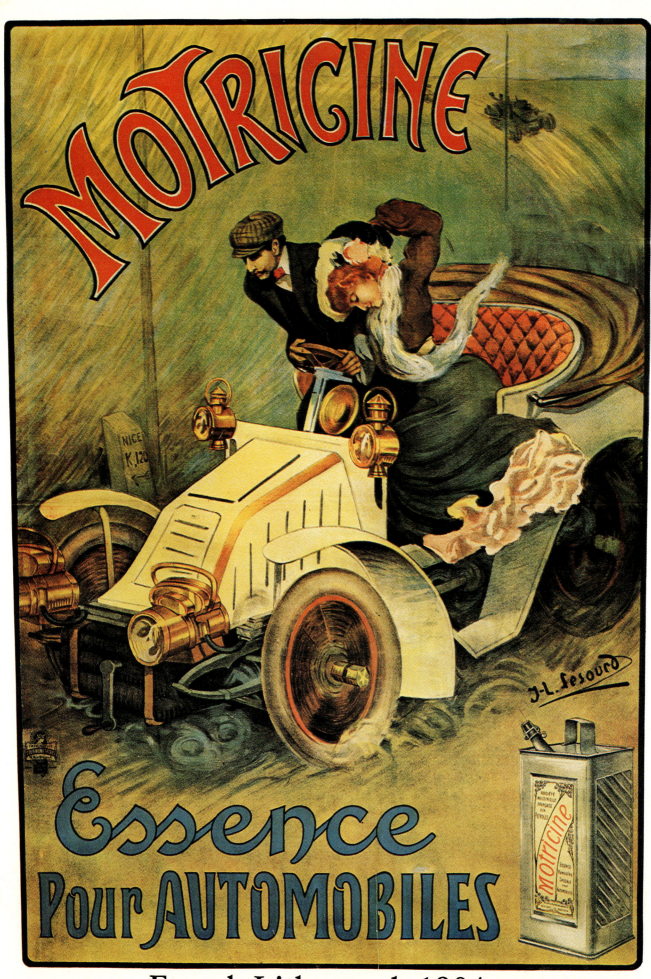

French Lithograph 1904

Fiat Corsa 1901

FIAT stood for Fabbrica Italiana Automobili Torino (founded 1899), and the capital letters were used until 1906 when it became Fiat. It was the first Italian firm to make a name in international motor sport and its first car designed specially for competition driving was this one, with a four-cylinder 24 hp engine of 6.4 litres which gave it a top speed of nearly 60 mph. It was also the first Fiat with an all-steel chassis rather than timber. Its early wins were in hill climbs. Vincenzo Lancia, the company's chief tester, won the Sassi Superga and Moncenisio hill climbs in it in 1902, when it also won Portugal's first motor race.

Renault 1906

The 1903 Paris–Madrid disaster had meant the end of inter-city races. But only three years later the French introduced a new kind of competition. It was held over two days at Le Mans, with six laps of a 64-mile circuit of public roads on each day, making a total of 769 miles. It was the first Grand Prix. Thirty-two cars of 13 makes from Germany, Italy and France competed in scorching heat. Renault had entered three red 90 hp cars with four-cylinder 13 litre engines — two-seaters, because riding mechanics were needed. Only one of the Renaults finished, but it won by less than one minute from a Fiat after nearly 12 hours driving at an average speed of 62.88 mph.

Italian 'FIAT' Advertisement

L'AQUILA ITALIANA au Tour de France
(AQUILA ITALIANA Fabbrica Automobili Torino)

1903 De Dietrich, product of a company that began by making railway locomotives, later known as Lorraine-Dietrich or simply Lorraine. It ended in 1935.

1904 Mercedes, built in Germany by a company which merged with Benz in 1926 to become Mercedes-Benz, which remains an honoured name.

1900 Napier, made in England by Montague Napier; Napiers closed in 1924.

Still Running

After more than 80 years a surprising number of veteran cars are still in running order, and many can be seen on a Sunday in November every year on the London–Brighton Run. The first run was held on November 14th, 1896, known as Emancipation Day, to mark the easing of restrictions that had hampered motoring in Britain and the lifting of the speed limit to 12 mph. Some 30 cars took part, most of them imported specially from the continent, their drivers braving the weather and hostile members of the public at a time when there were no garages and few signposts on the road. Today some two million people line the 52-mile route to watch the run, an annual event since 1927 except for wartime years. The pictures show some of the veterans on a recent run.

1904 De Dion-Bouton, made in France by Count de Dion and Georges Bouton. The last De Dion was made in 1932.

1895 Panhard-Levassor, built in France by a firm that originally made woodworking machines. The name died out in 1967.

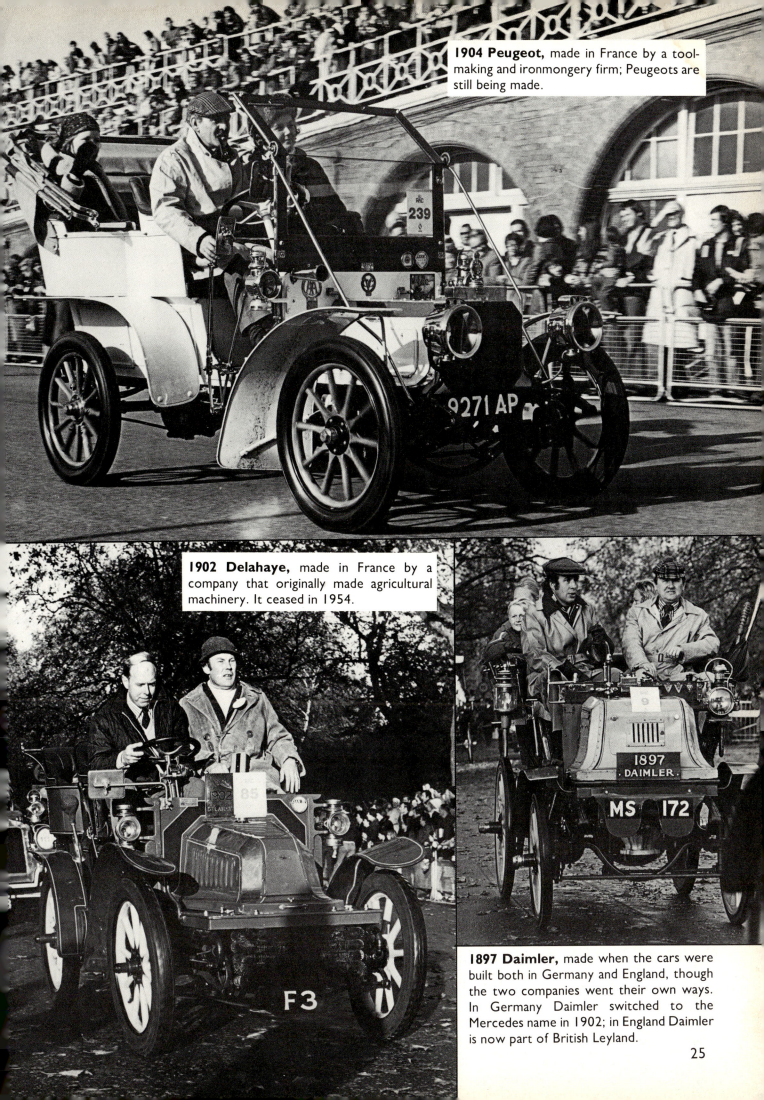

1904 Peugeot, made in France by a tool-making and ironmongery firm; Peugeots are still being made.

1902 Delahaye, made in France by a company that originally made agricultural machinery. It ceased in 1954.

1897 Daimler, made when the cars were built both in Germany and England, though the two companies went their own ways. In Germany Daimler switched to the Mercedes name in 1902; in England Daimler is now part of British Leyland.

25

Scorchers and Speedsters 1907–1916

In the quest for more power, engines continued to get larger until about 1911, when smaller but more efficient engines began to be seen. Georges Boillot won the French Grand Prix of 1912 in a Peugeot of 7.6 litres, beating a Fiat with an engine of almost twice the size into second place. In 1914 the race was won by a 4.5 litre Mercedes at an average speed only 5 mph slower than that of the 12.8 litre Merc. which had won in 1908. Yet until the start of World War One the car was still mainly a rich man's plaything and armies still relied on horses and mules. The war changed attitudes; by the end of it the internal combustion engine was powering ambulances and military vehicles of all kinds, and the tank had arrived.

Rover 1907

Britain's first regular series of motor races was the International Tourist Trophy, held from 1905 in the Isle of Man, the only place in Britain where racing was allowed on the roads. As the title indicated, the races were for touring cars, and the 1907 winner was this 20 hp Rover of 3.5 litres. It was a case of third time lucky for the Coventry company founded in 1904. In the 1905 TT its tourers had come fifth and twelfth. In 1906 they were excluded for late arrival. Twenty-two cars set out on the six-lap 240-mile race in 1907, of which only two finished, several running out of fuel on the tortuous, demanding circuit. The Rover finished in just under eight and a half hours at an average speed of 28.8 mph.

Hutton 1908

This car, built for the 1908 Isle of Man TT race, was actually a Napier, but by this time Napier was making and heavily publicising six-cylinder cars. So when J. E. Hutton, a Surrey motor distributor, asked the company to build him a four-cylinder for the TT race — which was restricted to four-cylinder cars — Napier was embarrassed. It built the car, and two others, looking like Napiers right to the water-cooling tower crowning the radiator, but insisted they must compete under the Hutton name. One of the three cars, which had 26 hp 5.7 litre engines and a top speed of 85 mph, won the race, adding to Napier's embarrassment (though the one Hutton drove himself failed to finish). Later a Hutton set records at Brooklands.

Rolls-Royce Silver Ghost

The car that earned Rolls-Royce the accolade: 'the best car in the world'. Strictly speaking, the name Silver Ghost applied to one specific car, pictured here, which was made in 1907 as the thirteenth of a series of six-cylinder 7 litre cars known as the 40/50 series (because of the engine type and power rating). It was painted silver and given silver-plated fittings, hence the name, though this has since come to be used for all the 40/50 cars made between 1906 and 1925. One Silver Ghost was driven from London to Edinburgh in 1911 entirely in top gear, and then lapped Brooklands at 78.26 mph. A single-seat version clocked 101 mph at Brooklands. The Silver Ghost gave performance with comfort and elegance.

Blitzen Benz

This chain-driven monster, the Blitzen (Lightning) Benz record breaker, had a four-cylinder 21.5 litre engine developing 200 hp. Victor Hemery lapped Brooklands in one at 127.88 mph in 1909, setting records that lasted beyond World War One. The car pictured was driven by Barney Oldfield in America at 131.72 mph in 1910, and Bob Burman drove it at 142.5 mph at Daytona Beach in 1911. I. G. 'Cupid' Hornsted took 27 records and won three races at Ostend with a Blitzen in 1914, and one of the giant cars was still being raced at Brooklands where it lapped at over 115 mph in 1930. A version was used by Field Marshal von Hindenberg in World War One.

Itala Peking–Paris

Races grew ever longer and more adventurous, the ultimate in marathons being the 1907 race from Peking, China, to Paris, France. Five cars set out on the 10,000-mile journey across deserts, swamps, rivers, mountain ranges and the wastelands of Siberia. For much of the way there were no roads and the cars drove along railway tracks — the Trans-Siberian in the picture. The winner, in 60 days, was Prince Scipio Borghese (wearing the pith helmet) in an Itala 35/45 of 7.4 litres, built by an Italian firm founded in 1904. Accompanied by Luigi Barzini, who covered the race for the *Daily Telegraph*, he finished three weeks ahead of the other finishers, two De Dions and a Dutch Spyker.

Fiat S76

A one-off 300 hp record-breaker, almost the biggest four-cylinder car ever made, the S76 had a 28.3 litre engine from an airship. The top of its bonnet was 5 ft. off the ground. Italian driver Pietro Bordino clocked 124 mph with it unofficially, at Salt-burn Sands in Yorkshire in 1911. Two years later Arthur Duray, an American-born Frenchman, drove it over a flying kilometre at Ostend at 132.37 mph, but that also failed to qualify as a record as he did not make a return run in the opposite direction.

Fiat S74

Almost the last of the chain-driven giants, the Fiat S74 had a four-cylinder engine of 14.1 litres giving 140 bhp; yet it was not the biggest car in the 1912 French Grand Prix at Dieppe as there was a Lorraine-Dietrich with an engine of over 15 litres in the 995-mile two-day event.

The three Fiats that took part were the fastest cars in the race. One of them, driven by American David Bruce-Brown, who had won the 1911 American Grand Prize in an S74, touched 101 mph before he was disqualified for an unscheduled stop for fuel. Louis Wagner, in another S74, finished second at an average of 67.32 mph behind a Peugeot.

Mercedes 90 hp

A mighty car with an engine of 9.6 litres — equal to those of nine superminis of modern times — the Mercedes 90 brought together the pointed radiator and the three-pointed star insignia that were to become the marque's recognition marks. One of the cars was shipped to America, where Italian-born Ralph De Palma led the Indianapolis 500-mile race of 1912 in it until a connecting rod broke two laps before the end. However, he then won the Vanderbilt Cup of that year at 68.97 mph. De Palma crashed the car in another race but rebuilt it in time to win the 1914 Vanderbilt at 75.49 mph. The early history of the car pictured is unknown, but it was discovered being used as a fire engine in Berkshire after World War Two, and has been lovingly restored to give a top speed of nearly 90 mph.

XK 3202

Lozier 1910

One of the best American performers of pre-World War One days was the Lozier, available in 46 hp four-cylinder and 50 hp six-cylinder form. They were excellent road-going cars but built with readily detachable lamps and wings for racing; there were also add-on fuel tanks for long-distance events. Apart from sponsoring works drivers, the company actively encouraged private owners to compete in local events, sending representatives to advise them. Six-cylinder 9 litre cars won the National Stock Car Championships in 1910 and the Vanderbilt Cup in 1911, in which year a Lozier also came second in the Indianapolis 500. But at the end of that year the company withdrew from racing. Like many small car firms it was finding it difficult to survive against the American giants and though it slashed prices it closed in 1917.

Buick

The start of a 10-mile sprint at the inaugural three-day meeting at Indianapolis, immediately after the opening of the two and a half mile long speedway track in 1909. The cars nearest the camera are Buicks; the company sent a works team of 15 cars with 40 drivers and mechanics to the meeting, and scored a one, two, three victory in the sprint, with Lewis Strang establishing a record at 66.93 mph. In the 250-mile main event Bob Burman in a Buick won at 53.77 mph, despite the fact that the surface of the track was breaking up. On another occasion Burman raced his Buick against a biplane, and won. Note that the cars then still had the steering wheel on the right-hand side.

Marmon Wasp

There was a crowd of 80,000 and the gates had to be shut an hour before the start of the first Indianapolis 500-mile race in 1911. The winner was a specially built, pointed-tail American car with a six-cylinder engine of 7.8 litres. Because of its yellow and black paint scheme it was originally called the Yellow Jacket but by the day of the race it had become the Wasp, because the word was shorter. It was driven by Ray Harroun, who completed the distance around the oval track in 6 hours 42 minutes at a speed of 74.59 mph. There were two unusual features about the car. First, it was a single-seater at a time when a riding mechanic was normally still carried. Second, because this meant the driver had no passenger able to look over his shoulder — which other drivers reckoned unsafe — Harroun fitted a rear-view mirror, the first one ever used.

Simplex 1914

One of the last chain-driven cars in America, the Simplex semi-racing runabout was made by the New York firm of Smith and Mabley, who had begun making cars in 1904 after importing Mercedes into the US. The 75 hp, near-10 litre open two-seater was capable of 80 mph, and while it was chain-driven it had the refinement of an electric starter. However, the firm ceased making cars during World War One.

Vauxhall Prince Henry

This was the car widely held to be the first production sports car — though the term had not come into use when it went on sale in 1911. It developed from a car which Laurence Pomeroy, Vauxhall's respected chief engineer, had designed a year earlier for the Prince Henry Trials, a series of annual reliability trials sponsored by Prince Heinrich of Prussia in which touring cars drove through Germany, Poland, Hungary and Austria. It had a 3 litre engine in a light, four-seat body without doors; three were built and were trouble free, though not winners. The production model Prince Henry had a four-cylinder 4 litre engine and could do 75 mph. It went on sale still without doors, though later it acquired small ones.

Hispano-Suiza Alfonso

A rival of the Vauxhall Prince Henry as one of the first catalogued sports cars was Spain's Hispano-Suiza Alfonso. The maker's name meant literally 'Spanish-Swiss' and came about because the cars were made in Barcelona but designed by a Swiss, Marc Birkigt. The name Alfonso was in honour of Spain's King Alfonso XIII, a motoring enthusiast who put up a cup for racing. The Alfonso was a replica of a successful racing voiturette of 1910, though with a bigger four-cylinder engine of 3.6 litres. It was capable of 80 mph and available in two wheelbase lengths — the shorter one for two-seat cars, the longer for four-seaters. It sold from 1911 to 1916 — and King Alfonso frequently drove one himself.

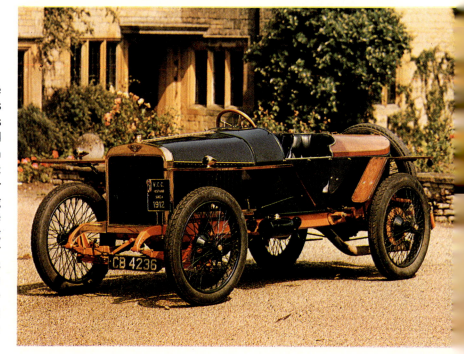

Stutz Bearcat

To young Americans before World War One this car was what the Thunderbird was to be to young Americans after World War Two — a hairy-chested virility symbol, the most sought-after of sports cars. Harry C. Stutz started by making racing cars in 1911 and then moved on to cars anyone could buy. The Bearcat, with a four-cylinder 6.4 litre engine, had two seats, no doors and no conventional windscreen, though there was a curious monocle screen mounted on the steering column. Bearcats were also raced; a team of three cars with 4.8 litre engines was introduced in 1915 under the name of the White Squadron and scored many victories in the following years.

Ford Model T Raceabout

The Model T was the world's best-selling car until its record was broken by the VW Beetle after World War Two. It sold more than 15 million between 1908 and 1927, the product of a new age of mass production. It also made history by being the first American car to have its steering wheel on the left-hand side, even though Americans had always driven on the right of the road. The Model T had a rugged four-cylinder 2.9 litre engine, two forward gears plus reverse, and a hand throttle. It was simple to strip and repair and, apart from body styles, it changed little over the years except that it got cheaper. With a speed of around 40 mph it was not a speedster, but it was to be found everywhere and in 1909 a stripped Model T won a New York–Seattle race (in a time of 22 days) and models like this 1914 Raceabout competed on American tracks.

Austin 1908

Herbert Austin quit the Wolseley company in 1908 to start his own firm at Longbridge, Birmingham, and having competed in the Paris–Vienna race of 1908 it was natural for him to move into racing, building three cars for the 1908 Grand Prix held in Dieppe. They had six-cylinder 9.6 litre engines of 100 bhp, which were the second smallest in the race, most having 12 or 13 litres, and the highest-placed Austin was one driven by J.T.C. Moore-Brabazon (later Lord Brabazon of Tara) which finished 18th. That had shaft drive, whereas the other two Austins were chain driven. The two Austins that finished were the only British cars to do so, but they never raced again, being basically fast tourers. In the car shown is Jack Johnson who began his seven-year reign as world heavyweight boxing champion in 1908.

Audi Alpensieger

After working for Karl Benz, August Horch started his own car firm in Germany in 1900. However, he parted from the company that bore his name in 1909 after disagreements with his partners, and started another. Being barred from using the name Horch he called the new company Audi, which is a Latinised form of the same name. He had early success driving his new cars in the Austrian Alpine Trials and in 1912 introduced the Audi Type C14/35PS, a 3.6 litre 40 bhp sports car with aluminium bodywork, which carried off team awards in the Alpine Trials of 1913 and 1914, hence the name Alpensieger. Horch is seen at the wheel after the 1914 victory.

Mercedes GP 1914

The French Grand Prix of 1914 was the first to be run under an engine size regulation. (It was 4.5 litres.) It was also the first in which team tactics were seen. The favourite was Georges Boillot in a Peugeot, who had won the previous year; but Mercedes entered five cars capable of 112 mph and expended one of them in pressuring Boillot. After his car blew up on the final lap Mercedes came in first, second and third, with Christian Lautenschlager the winner at an average of 65.66 mph. The victory won little applause from the French spectators; the race was just four weeks before the start of World War One.

The Open Road 1918–1930

Now the car became an everyday form of transport for millions of people both in their work and in their leisure time. The open road beckoned. Car bonnets grew longer, wheels smaller, bodies lower and brakes came to all four wheels. Cars continued to get smaller, particularly in Britain where a horsepower tax made big cars expensive to run. (The tax on a Rolls-Royce Silver Ghost was £45 a year.) This led to the popularity of cars of around 10 hp. In Grand Prix racing progressive restrictions to curb speeds brought engines down to 2 litres in size, though constructors compensated for this by the use of superchargers, and bigger cars like the great green Bentleys thundered around Le Mans in sports car races. However, the Depression that affected much of the world in 1929 was to make economy even more desirable.

Bentley 3 Litre

W. O. Bentley's first car, the massive but elegant four-cylinder 3 litre went on sale in 1921, and two years later the Twenty Four Hours endurance race for sports and touring cars began at Le Mans. The names of Bentley and Le Mans were to become closely linked. In 1924 John Duff and Frank Clement won the race in a privately entered Bentley at 53.78 mph, after which W.O. began entering works teams — without success until 1927. In that year's race all three works Bentleys were involved in a crash during the night. Two were written off; the third, driven by Dr. Dudley Benjafield and Sammy Davis, had a broken wheel, a bent front axle and frame, a broken headlamp and a cracked steering arm joint. But it was patched up as far as possible and they drove on, running through the night on one headlamp, and eventually won at 61.35 mph. The publicity helped sell more than 1,600 3 litres. Reliability was their great claim, and Bentley was so confident of it that he gave a five-year guarantee on mechanical parts.

Bentley 4½ Litre

The first of Bentley's bigger-engined cars made its debut at Le Mans in 1927, but was wrecked in a multiple pile-up at the White House Corner. The following year three were entered and the 4.5 litre driven by Woolf Barnato and Bernard Rubin won at 69.11 mph, while in 1929 4.5 litre cars came second and third behind a new, bigger Bentley, the 6.5 litre, which won again in 1930. A number of 4.5 litre cars were supercharged and one driven by Sir Henry 'Tim' Birkin pushed the Brooklands lap record to 137.96 mph in 1931. But by then Bentley had withdrawn officially from racing; the company had collapsed and control had passed to Rolls-Royce.

Vauxhall 30/98

The only other British production car that was any kind of a match for the 4.5 litre Bentley in 1927 was this four-cylinder 4.2 litre with the distinctive fluted Vauxhall bonnet. The car first went on sale after World War One with a 4.5 litre engine but was redesigned in 1923. Its origins went back to 1913 when designer Laurence Pomeroy was asked to build a car to win a hill climb. He bored out the engine of a Prince Henry, and put it in a new body, naming it the 30/98 for reasons no one has ever fathomed. It won the climb, and after the war was sold as 'A very refined fast touring car capable of high speeds and suitable for competition work'. It was the fastest car produced in quantity, guaranteeing 85 mph on the road and 100 mph in Brooklands trim. Vauxhall sold 586 before they were taken over by General Motors in 1926 and the factory switched to more mundane models.

Crossley 20/70

The bowler-hatted driver is the Crossley sales manager of the time, A. M. Robertson. The 3.8 litre was a winner, and at £875 it was cheap compared with the Bentley 3 litre or the Vauxhall 30/98. It featured a three-compartment rear end which enabled it to be sold in two or four-seat versions recommended for fast touring; it was guaranteed to reach 75 mph. Brakes were available on the front wheels for an extra £35. Leon Cushman drove two pale blue tourers from the Manchester works to Brooklands in 1924 and in three events on the same day scored a first, a second and a third place.

Lancia Lambda

Vincenzo Lancia, a racing driver before he founded the Lancia company in Italy, made some 13,000 Lambda cars, both saloons and tourers, between 1923 and 1931. They were remarkably advanced cars for the time, having a unitary chassis and body which enabled the car to be lower than any other of its size. They also had independent front suspension, an alloy cylinder block, brakes on all four wheels, pump cooling and a detachable hard top was available for the tourers. The original V4 engine of 2.1 litres gave a speed of over 70 mph; the 2.5 litre engine introduced in 1928 gave more than 80 mph.

Renault Routier Du Desert

At the start of the Twenties Citroen built a car with caterpillar half-tracks instead of wheels, which became the first motor vehicle to cross the Sahara desert. In 1923 the rival French firm of Renault built another answer to the problem of crossing the desert. This relied on wheels, twelve in all, six sets of twinned ones, with the rear four pairs driven by the 13.9 hp four-cylinder engine. A husband and wife drove one across Africa in 1925, but the problem remained that the Renault, while fine on roads, still got stuck in sand; the Citroen made lighter work of sand but lurched slowly on roads. What was wanted was a Jeep, but that was still in the future.

Benz
Tropfenwagen

This Grand Prix car was years ahead of its time, which was 1923. Designed by Edmund Rumpler, it had a six-cylinder 2 litre engine at the rear, in which it was the forerunner of Auto Union, Cooper Climax and other racers of the future. It had a modern-looking aerodynamic body with a crescent-shaped radiator above the engine, and during tests the 'Teardrop' even sprouted aerofoils on bonnet and tail to help hold it on the road. Its speed was around 110 mph. It appeared only once in a major race, the first Grand Prix de l'Europe at Monza in 1923, for which three cars were entered and two finished fourth and fifth, though one ran later as a roadster. But in 1926 Benz merged with Mercedes.

Alvis 12/50

The Alvis firm was founded in Coventry in 1919 but by 1924 it was near collapse; it was saved by the introduction of the four-cylinder 1.5 litre 12/50 model with its beetle-back tail. It was designed by the company's chief engineer, Capt. Smith-Clarke, who lightened it by boring holes everywhere possible, not only in the chassis but even through the pedals and handbrake. In 1923 a prototype driven by Major C. M. Harvey won a 200-mile race at Brooklands at 93.29 mph, despite having been rebuilt after being almost gutted by fire five days earlier. By 1928 production was running at 900 a year and five modified cars with front-wheel drive ran at Le Mans in 1929, one of them scoring a class win at 59 mph.

Morgan

Known affectionately as a Moggie, this inexpensive three-wheeler — its single wheel was at the back — was the best known in the world. Its air-cooled V-twin engine of 1.1 litres right out in front of the bonnet could drive (by chain) the standard version at 70 mph, while the Aero or Super Sports of the late Twenties, the model pictured, was 10 mph faster. It had better roadholding and was safer than most three-wheelers. Its two-seat body was light and it had a comparatively high performance. It was seen in trials, sprints and hill climbs and raced at Brooklands, though for a number of years it was allowed only in motorcycle events. (It was also shown at motorcycle rather than motor shows.) Made at Malvern, Worcs, by a family firm founded in 1910, it was later to acquire electric starting, a three-speed gearbox in place of a two-speed, and a four-cylinder engine.

Fiat Mephistopheles

Originally this car was a racer with an 18.1 litre engine, first seen at Brooklands in 1908, when Felice Nazzaro brought it to England to race against a 20 litre Napier Samson. The Fiat won at 121.64 mph, and went on racing at Brooklands until 1922 when John Duff blew the engine. Ernest Eldridge then acquired it and lengthened the chassis by 18 inches to accommodate a 21.7 litre six-cylinder airship engine. In 1924, on a tree-lined road at Arpajon, near Paris, it took the world land speed record to 146.01 mph. This was the last time the record was ever created on a road.

Fiat 806 Corsa

This was Fiat's last racing car; racing was becoming too specialised a field for major companies interested in volume sales of cars for the road. Only one car was built, and it ran only once — but it won the race. That was the 1927 Milan Grand Prix, and it won at an average speed of 94.57 mph. Pietro Bordino drove the car with its 12 cylinder 1.5 litre engine in the race run under Formula Libre (unlimited size) rules and beat bigger engined Alfas and Bugattis, but then Fiat withdrew from racing and the car vanished. Rumour had it that the car was destroyed because it had been built without the authority of the firm's directors.

Sunbeam, Bluebird

The Twenties were the heyday of record-breaking. In 1923 Malcolm (later Sir Malcolm) Campbell bought a Sunbeam in which Kenelm Lee Guinness had pushed the world land speed record to 133.75 mph at Brooklands a year before. It had a V12 aircraft engine of 13.8 litres developing 350 bhp. Campbell fitted it with a new body and longer tail and called it Bluebird, a name he was to give to all his record breakers. By the start of 1924 he had twice beaten Guinness's speed, but on neither occasion had his speed been recorded properly and by this time Ernest Eldridge in a Fiat had reached 146.01 mph. But on Pendine sands, Carmarthenshire, Campbell achieved 146.16 mph and in 1925 raised this to 150.87 mph.

Sunbeam, Tiger

By comparison with Bluebird, Major (later Sir) Henry Segrave's Sunbeam Tiger had a tiny engine of only 4 litres. It was a supercharged V12 unit, created by combining two six-cylinder Grand Prix engine blocks, but it gave 300 bhp and in 1926 Segrave pushed the record up to 152.31 mph. The Tiger was the last world land speed record car to be raced; subsequent ones were designed simply to go fast in a straight line. The Tiger was to win a race at Brooklands in 1928 at more than 128 mph. With its sister car Tigress — only the two were built — it also ran in speed trials and hill climbs.

Thomas Special, Babs

Welsh driver Parry Thomas, known as 'the Flying Celt', set out to beat Segrave's record by putting a 120 cylinder, 27 litre, 400 bhp Liberty aero engine on the chassis of a Higham Special, naming the car Babs. On Pendine sands in 1926 he took the recod to 160.30 mph

and in 1927 to 171.02. But Campbell had built a new Bluebird and replied with 174.88 mph. Thomas went back to Pendine and was travelling at nearly 170 mph when the offside driving chain broke, smashed through the windscreen and decapitated him, after which Babs turned over and burst into flames. It was buried beneath the sand, where it remained until it was exhumed in the Seventies.

Sunbeam 1000 hp

Segrave had Sunbeam build him a new car in which he sat between two 500 hp Matabele aircraft engines. Each was a 12 cylinder of 22.4 litres; the combined brake horsepower was 1,000. There was one radiator in front of the forward engine, two on the rear engine. The 23.5 ft. long body of the car was made of aluminium sheets and the total weight was three tons. At Daytona Beach in Florida, on his first run, his brakes failed and he had to drive into the sea to stop. But before 1927 was out he became the first man to beat the 'double ton' at a speed of 203.79 mph.

Irving-Napier, Golden Arrow

By 1929 the world land speed record was held by America's Ray Keech, who had reached 207.5 mph in a car with three Liberty engines giving a total capacity of 81 litres! Segrave had a new car designed by Capt. Jack

Irving, 3 ft. 9 in. high and housing a 12 cylinder 930 hp Napier Lion engine of a type used in a Schneider Cup-winning aircraft. There were rifle-type sights along the bonnet so that Segrave could aim the car at a distant landmark. At Daytona, despite wet sand, he achieved 231.44 mph and on his return was knighted by King George V, but was killed a year later in a boat, just after setting a new water speed record.

Ettore Bugatti, Italian-born but manufacturing in France, built small cars with the precision of fine watches and they outperformed much bigger cars. He made tourers and racers with distinctive horseshoe radiators, all readily available to would-be competitors, unlike the racers of some factories which were supplied only to works or selected drivers. Noted for their speed, but rarely for their braking, Bugattis dominated motor sport through the Twenties and in the early Thirties.

Bugatti Type 13

It took ten years for Bugatti's first significant car to win its popular name, the Brescia. He had begun producing the little car in 1910 and though it had only a 1.4 litre engine, Ernst Friderich drove one into second place behind a Fiat of more than 10 litres in a race in France in 1911. But there were then few races for voiturettes — the interest was in big cars — and World War One caused it to be mothballed. Then in 1921 the first Italian Grand Prix had a voiturette class and Bugattis came in first, second, third and fourth, with Friderich the winner at 72 mph. The Grand Prix was held at Brescia and the name stuck to the car. Two thousand Brescia racers and tourers were eventually made, the later ones with 1.5 litre engines. Two of the most famous were Cordon Rouge and Cordon Bleu, which Raymond Mays modified to exceed 90 mph and drove in hill climbs and sprints.

Bugatti Type 35

In 1924 Bugatti brought out his first eight-cylinder car, the finest sports car of the Twenties. The standard car had a 2 litre engine but there were a number of versions, including the 35B with a 2.3 litre supercharged engine which was capable of 125 mph. The cars won Grands Prix everywhere and were the most numerous and most successful cars of the late Twenties, winning more than two thousand awards in all. From the Type 35 developed the Type 43 of 1928, a passenger car longer, wider and less powerful, though it had a top speed of 112 mph. Essentially a racing car with a touring body, it was one of the fastest road-going cars of the day.

Bugatti Type 45

A revolutionary 16 cylinder car, this had its power unit formed by the use of two Type 35 engines geared together, each bank then being fitted with a rear-mounted supercharger. Only three were made, and were used in hill climbs in 1930. The chassis was used a year later for the Type 54, a near-5 litre Grand Prix car which had little success by Bugatti standards, though in 1933 Graf Czaykowski set a one-hour record in a Type 54 at 132.87 mph. Later in the year he was killed when the car crashed after skidding on oil in the Italian Grand Prix at Monza.

Bugatti Type 51

By the end of the Twenties more power was required in Grand Prix racing and Bugatti built his first car with twin overhead camshafts on an eight-cylinder 2.3 litre engine. It was launched in 1931 and won the Monaco, Tunis and Belgian Grands Prix among other successes. Again there were several versions, such as the Type 51A which was a supercharged 1.5 litre model that won at Monaco and elsewhere until it was overtaken by the Alfa Romeo Monopostos. From it also evolved the Type 55, a two-seater sports car with flaring wings and the 2.3 litre engine. It was a great roadster, capable of 50 mph in first gear, 75 mph in second, 100 mph in third and 115 mph in top.

Bugatti Type 41 Royale

It was a car for kings, said Ettore Bugatti, of this giant limousine which made its debut in 1927. It was around 22 ft. long, depending on the coachwork chosen, and weighed two and a half tons. It had an eight-cylinder engine of 12.8 litres designed for aircraft (and later used in French railcars). It could exceed 100 mph with ease, but drank petrol at the rate of 6–8 mpg. It was the biggest, heaviest and most expensive production car in the world. Actually no king ever bought one. Over a six-year period only six were made out of an intended production of 25. One was sold in England, one in France and one in Germany, while three were run by the Bugatti family.

Opel Rak 2

To say this car went like a rocket was literally true, for it was fitted with 24 gunpowder rockets at the tail which the driver fired in stages. There were short wings at the sides to exert a downward thrust. The brave pilot of this explosive machine was Fritz Opel, who demonstrated it on the Avus track in Germany in 1928, and lived to tell the tale. In fact it worked and he achieved a speed of 125 mph, though the car had no future.

Auburn Speedster

Named after the town in Indiana where they were made from 1900, Auburn cars were generally staid until 1924 when the company was bought by Errett Lobban Cord, who introduced models that were anything but staid. The two-seat Speedster of 1928 was a high-speed long-distance cruiser with a distinctive boat-style rear end and exhaust pipes emerging through the side of the bonnet. The engine was an eight-cylinder 4.5 litre Lycoming of 90 bhp, though some later versions had a supercharged V12.

Grandes Marques 1931–1941

The Depression cut the production of cars, particularly in America, and also reduced the number of racing cars, which resulted in a temporary free-for-all as race organisers created their own regulations according to the cars available. Recovery in the mid-Thirties was accompanied by an upsurge of nationalism in motor sport. Hitler in Germany and Mussolini in Italy offered subsidies and prizes to their motor manufacturers to produce cars that would bring kudos by vanquishing those of other countries. This brought about such powerful racers from those countries that other nations switched to light car competitions. At the same time, Germany and Italy built motorways, resulting in roadsters higher geared than in countries like Britain with its tortuous roads. But World War Two ended production of private cars and racers.

Cord 810

Errett Lobban Cord was a showman and his cars were flamboyant eye-catchers. The Cord 810 with its alligator-like bonnet, wraparound grille and headlamps that retracted into the front wings was chosen by the New York Museum of Modern Art as an outstanding example of industrial design. The car was also mechanically advanced for 1935, with front-wheel drive and electric pre-selection of gear ratios, the fourth of which was an overdrive. The V8 engine of 4.7 litres gave 125 bhp and a speed of 90 mph, while the Cord 812, a supercharged version introduced in 1937, was capable of 112 mph. Some 2,500 of the two models were built before Cord's empire foundered in 1937, and other manufacturers made replicas in the Sixties.

Duesenberg SJ

E. L. Cord also controlled Auburn and Duesenberg, and when he took over the latter firm in 1928 he directed Fred Duesenberg to produce a car that would outperform anything on the roads of America. The result was the Model J with a 6.9 litre engine developing 265 bhp, about twice the power of any other American car, and with a speed of 115 mph. Then in 1932 came the SJ (S for supercharged) which gave 320 bhp, making it the most powerful production car in the world. Normal top speed was nearly 130 mph, but Ab Jenkins drove one at 152 mph in 1935. All the bodies were custom built and owners included Clark Gable and Gary Cooper, but fewer than 500 of the two models were made before the Cord collapse.

Cadillac Fleetwood

While the Cord cars had glamour and razzmatazz, the Cadillac was identified with dignity and prestige. While the Cord cars suited film stars and foreign princelings the Cadillac was the car for bankers and their families. The Cadillac Fleetwood was the most completely luxurious and prestigious car it was possible to buy in the Thirties, according to the advertising. There were three engine sizes, a V8 of 5.1 litres, a V12 of 6 litres and a V16 of 7.4 litres, and thirteen different body styles, and for all its conservative image Cadillac was not slow to embrace new ideas. It introduced power braking in 1931, ride control in 1932, a no-draught ventilation system in 1933, independent front suspension in 1934 and the steering column gear change in 1938.

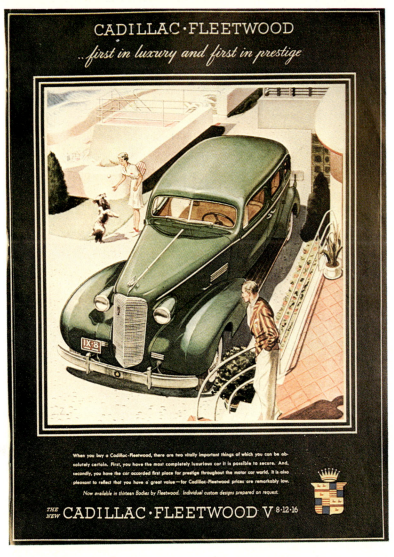

SSI

SS stood for Swallow Sports, a Coventry company which began by making motorcycle sidecars and then special bodies for popular cars such as the Austin Seven. The SSI was in 1931 its first complete car and the ancestor of the Jaguar. Basically it was a Standard 16 hp car and kept its six-cylinder 2 litre engine and other components, but engine and chassis had been lowered and there was a coupé body with a longer bonnet. In road tests by a motoring magazine it topped 62 other cars in speed, acceleration and braking. "A thousand pound car priced at £325" declared the advertising, and the combination of good looks, performance and comparatively low cost was to remain the company's formula for years to come. The SS90 in 1935 was a short chassis two-seater version with a 2.5 litre engine.

Jensen 3.5 Litre

Like William Lyons, the brothers Alan and Richard Jensen also began by making better bodies for other company's cars, among them the Wolseley Hornet. The first car to emerge from their works in West Bromwich, Staffordshire, under the Jensen name was this Anglo-American hybrid of 1937. The body — available in both saloon and open sports versions — was by the brothers; the engine was an American Ford V8 of 3.6 litres. The car was also available with a bigger eight-cylinder Nash engine of 4.2 litres and was capable of 85 mph with either. Jensen was to become another respected name, particularly for the handsome styling of its coachwork.

SS Jaguar 100

The name Jaguar first appeared on this 1936 two-seater, though the SS prefix was to remain until the first postwar cars, by which time the initials had unpleasant associations with the Nazis. Again based on a Standard, the car was another good looker, wide and low with flared wings and a folding screen, and a six-cylinder 2.5 litre engine that gave it a speed of 90 mph. By 1938 there was also a 3.5 litre version capable of 105 mph — a rare speed at the time — and with 0–60 acceleration of 10.4 seconds. This car became a collector's item, for it held the real promise of what was to come from the firm of William (later Sir William) Lyons.

MG Midget

MG stood for Morris Garages, a Morris-owned firm distributing its cars in the Oxford area, which began modifying standard models and then producing cars behind the MG badge at the end of the Twenties. There were many models of the MG Midget in the Thirties, most of them open two-seaters with ash-framed, steel-clad bodies based on the Morris Minor and its 847 cc engine. Top speeds were in the seventies and they were not very comfortable, but they looked sporting and were coveted by every red-blooded young man in Britain. The biggest sellers were the J Type of the early Thirties and the P Type of the mid-Thirties, both of which sold around 2,500, establishing MG's style and tradition as Britain's most popular sports car.

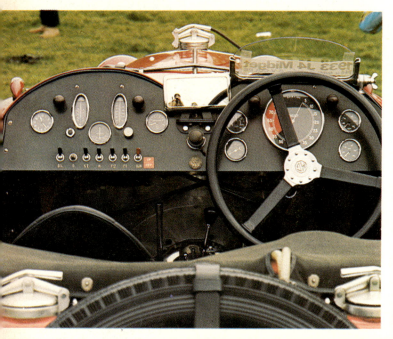

Aston Martin Le Mans

The prestigious Aston Martin firm began modestly as motor repairers in South London where Lionel Martin, one of the co-founders, rebuilt standard Singers as sports cars. (The 'Aston' part of the name came from Aston Clinton, the hill climb venue, where Martin raced them.) Like many others, the firm then moved on to making its own cars, with little success until the introduction of its International model in 1930. This was a 1.5 litre car which could be supplied in two chassis lengths and a variety of body styles equipped, according to the advertising, for road racing anywhere in the world. Class wins by specially prepared cars at Le Mans in 1931 and 1932 led to the Le Mans replica in 1933, a production car based on the successful racers but lighter and quicker with 85 mph performance. The Le Mans was distinguished by an outside exhaust and a slab fuel tank at the rear.

Monaco GP 1931

MG Montlhery

A version strictly for competition work was the MG C Type known as the Montlhery, which was introduced in 1931. This was a production racer, based on the D Type, with its engine reduced in size to bring it within the 750 cc class. The first batch was delivered in time for the 1931 Double Twelve race at Brooklands, a two-day event involving 24 hours' racing which was Britain's nearest equivalent to the Le Mans 24 hours race. MGs took the first five places, the winning car being shared by the Earl of March (later the Duke of Richmond) and Chris Staniland and averaging 65.62 mph. The car could be bought with or without supercharging (£295 unblown) and it was necessary only to remove lights and wings to turn it from a competition sports car into a stark racer or record breaker. Almost every British racing driver of note competed in one at some time.

Talbot 105

Swiss-born Georges Roesch designed high-quality sports cars which were made in Talbot's London factory during the Thirties, the most successful of which was the 105, introduced in 1931. It had a six-cylinder 3 litre engine giving 100 bhp and 90 mph in standard form, 140 bhp in tuned form, though Roesch set his face against super-charging which limited its successes in competitions.

Even so, 105s came first, second and third in their class in the Brooklands 500 mile race of 1931, and they also carried off the team prize in the Alpine Trial for three years running. Coachwork was available to the customer's choice and the 105 was seen not only as a sports car but as a four-seat saloon. It led to the Talbot 110, a 3.4 litre car, in 1936, but by this time Talbot had been taken over by the Rootes brothers and the company's range changed.

Brough Superior

George Brough was a perfectionist who made motorcycles known as 'the Rolls-Royce of motorcycles' in Nottingham. His first prototype for a car wore the number-plate 'GB 1933', combining his initials and the year. The car pictured was his first production model, demonstrated in 1935. It was an Anglo-American hybrid, one of a number at the time, using a British-made body with an American chassis and engine, a Hudson eight-cylinder of 4.1 litres, and a British-made drophead coupé body, distinguished by its heart-shaped radiator with vertical slats and cooling vents along the side of the bonnet. Brough followed this model with one using a six-cylinder 3.5 litre Hudson engine and his last was a V12 saloon in 1938, but then he switched to making munitions for war. His cars, with remarkable acceleration, were to be highly regarded by connoisseurs, but only a few were built.

Fiat 508S Balilla

During the Depression Fiat had abandoned its big, expensive models to concentrate on smaller, cheaper ones, the smallest being the 508, a 995 cc tourer, seating three with the use of a dickey seat, introduced in 1932. It had a top speed approaching 60 mph and was given the name 'Balilla' meaning 'Plucky little one'. It was to sell some 80,000. The 508S, a tuned version with a tail fin behind the cockpit, was introduced in 1933. A two-seat sports car capable of 75 mph, it was used in trials, rallies and under-1100 cc races, and provided the main opposition to small British sports cars. Around 2,000 were sold, including some made under licence by Simca in France and NSU in Germany.

Railton Light Sports Tourer

"Acceleration unequalled by anything on the road" boasted the advertisements. The Railton could get from 0 to 60 mph in an eye-blinking nine seconds. It could reach 80 mph in the second of its three gears and 107 in top. It was based on an Anglo-American four-seater built in Edinburgh by Noel Macklin, which used an eight-cylinder 4.2 litre Hudson engine and normally had a 0 to 60 acceleration time of 13 seconds and a top speed of 85 mph. Reid Railton, designer of the Brooklands Riley and other fast cars, modified this in 1936 to give 124 bhp instead of its normal 113, and made it a very potent car.

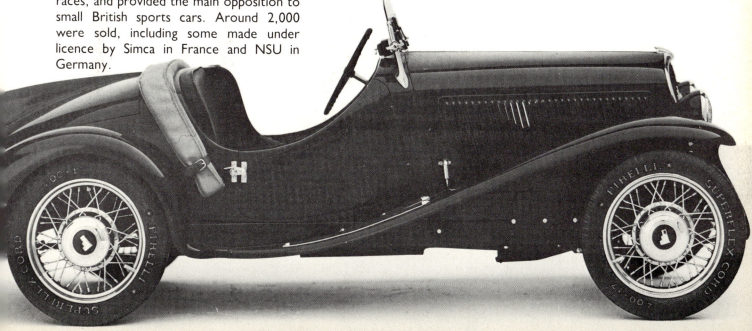

Alfa Romeo 6C1500

Vittorio Jano designed this sports two-seater in the late Twenties but its influence extended well into the Thirties. In its original standard form with a six-cylinder 1.5 litre engine it was capable of 70 mph, but the Super Sport version of 1929 with an optional supercharger, pictured here, could reach 87 mph. The car then grew into the 6C1750 with a bigger engine of 1.7 litres. This took the first three places in the Mille Miglia of 1930 and in fact won all the great sports car races of the time except Le Mans. Then Jano moved on to eight-cylinder cars.

Alfa Romeo Monza

The Alfa 8C2300 was known as the Monza because it made its debut there at the Italian Grand Prix of 1931, and Giuseppe Campari and Tazio Nuvolari won the 10-hour race at 96.17 mph. Descended from the 6C1750 sports car, it had an eight-cylinder super-charged engine of 2.3 litres, enlarged to 2.6 litres from 1933 by the Scuderia Ferrari, which went on racing it with many successes even after Alfa Romeo itself had withdrawn from racing. It was unable to match the resources of the heavily state-subsidised German factories, which Hitler was determined to make supreme.

Alfa Romeo 158

When Grand Prix racing eventually became a Nazi propaganda benefit the Italians, the British and others moved into voiturette racing under a 1.5 litre formula, where competition was still open. The 158, dubbed the Alfetta, had an eight-cylinder engine giving almost 200 bhp and enjoyed a successful first year in 1938 until Mercedes moved into that class too. But after improvements to the supercharging the cars were virtually undefeated and carried on winning after World War Two into the Fifties, as the 159.

Brooklands
Poster 1932

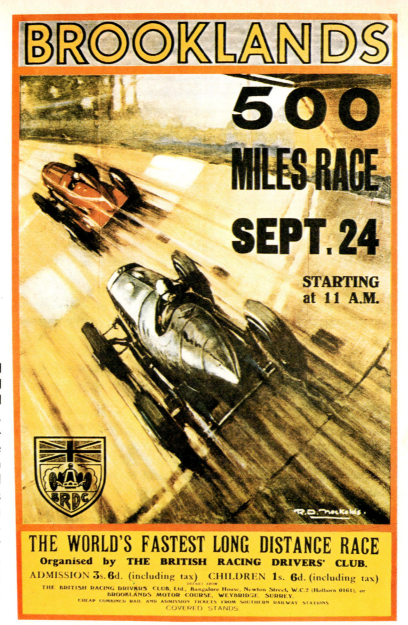

Alfa Romeo
Monoposto

This was the successor to the Monza and Europe's first successful single-seat Grand Prix car. Although riding mechanics had been dispensed with in the mid-Twenties, racing cars were still generally made as two-seaters until the advent of this car, the greatest of Vittorio Jano's designs. It had an eight-cylinder 2.6 litre engine and two small superchargers giving 215 bhp, and made its debut in the Italian Grand Prix of 1932 when Tazio Nuvolari beat off Alfa's Italian arch-rivals, the Maseratis, to win the five-hour event at 104.1 mph. The engine was enlarged steadily, to 2.9 litres, then 3.2 and finally 3.8 litres, and it won races everywhere until it was outclassed by the German cars.

Mercedes-Benz W125

Spurred on by grants from Hitler, two German car companies — Mercedes-Benz and Auto Union — competed ferociously in the second half of the Thirties, first one and then the other dominating major races. Their duel reached its climax with this Mercedes, the most powerful Grand Prix car ever built. Its eight-cylinder engine of 5.7 litres was supercharged to give 640 bhp and nearly 200 mph. Driven mainly by Hermann Lang, Rudolf Caracciola and Manfred von Brauchitsch, the cars won seven out of 13 events entered in 1937 including the German, Italian, Swiss and Monaco GPs. But speeds had become so alarming that for 1938 the authorities limited supercharged engines to 3 litres.

Auto Union D Type

Auto Union was a combination of the Audi, Horch, Wanderer and DKW companies, which still produced roadsters under their own names. This was the last of Auto Union's great racing cars, built for the new 3 litre formula, with a twelve-cylinder supercharged engine giving 400 bhp and a speed of around 185 mph. The last pre-war Grand Prix, held in Belgrade, was also Auto Union's last race, for when Germany was divided after World War Two its factory came within the Russian zone.

Auto Union Rekordwagen

The rivalry between Mercedes-Benz and Auto Union also extended to record breaking. In 1938 Rudolf Caracciola of Mercedes set a new Class B record of 268 mph for the flying kilometre; Bernd Rosemeyer of Auto Union — he never raced any other make of car — took on the task of breaking it. Ferdinand Porsche designed this streamliner for the bid on the Frankfurt autobahn. But when Rosemeyer was doing 260 mph a gust of wind caught the car, which crashed into a bridge, killing the driver instantly.

ERA

The acronym represented English Racing Automobile and the car was built in 1934 by Raymond Mays and Peter Berthon to compete against Continental opposition in the 1.5 litre voiturette class. Reid Railton designed the chassis and the engine was a Riley-based supercharged six-cylinder. Altogether 19 ERAs from A to E type were built at Bourne in Lincolnshire before the war, the most famous being Romulus, a B type given to Prince Birabongse of Siam as a 21st birthday present. Driving it under the name 'B. Bira' he scored 10 firsts and 13 places in 30 starts between 1936 and 1939, and also enjoyed success with a twin car named Remus. Raymond Mays' own car was outstanding in hill climbs and led Mays and Berthon to create the postwar BRM (British Racing Motor) which at first was spectacularly less successful.

Lagonda M45

"Overweight and underpowered" was a common criticism at the start of the Thirties of the cars built at Staines by a firm founded by an American named Wilbur Gunn. The M45, introduced in 1933, changed Lagonda's image, for although the car had a heavy body, usually a convertible in two-seat sports or four-seat tourer form, its six-cylinder 4.5 litre Meadows engine could drive it at up to 90 mph. In 1935 a racing version won Le Mans at 77.85 mph, ending a four-year run of victories by Alfa Romeo. In the same year W. O. Bentley, whose own company had been taken over by Rolls-Royce, joined the firm as chief engineer and his improvements made the car considerably fiercer.

BMW 328

One of the most successful sports cars of all time, the BMW 328 with its faired headlamps and flowing lines was remarkably modern in appearance in 1936; it was also quiet and comfortable by comparison with most sports cars of the time. Yet even in full road-going trim it could see off many stripped racing machines. Built of alloy panels on an ash frame, and with an undertray to improve its aerodynamics, it had a six-cylinder 2 litre engine and could reach 95 mph in standard form, 120 mph tuned. Sammy Davis drove one 102.23 miles in an hour at Brooklands in 1937. It had class wins in the Mille Miglia in 1938 and outright victory in the 1940 event; it also had a class win at Le Mans in 1939. About 450 were made and were still competitive after the war, when the engine was also used to power Bristol cars.

Monaco Race Poster

MONACO
2 AVRIL 1934

6ème GRAND PRIX AUTOMOBILE

Railton-Mobil

Sir Malcolm Campbell pushed the world speed record past 300 mph in 1935 and George Eyston took it to 345 mph in 1938; then later that year John Cobb unveiled this car designed by Reid Railton. It had two twelve-cylinder 24 litre Napier Lion engines, each developing 1250 bhp when super-charged. The nearside engine drove the front wheels and the offside engine the rear, while Cobb sat right up in the nose of the three-ton car beneath a streamlined body shell which could be detached in one piece. Cobb lifted the record to 350.20 mph in 1938 and to 369.70 mph on the eve of war in 1939. After the war — in 1947 — he returned to Utah and achieved 394.20 mph, a record which lasted until 1964, though he was killed on Loch Ness in 1952, trying to break the world water speed record.

Jeep

The outstanding performer of the war years, its chunky tyres and four-wheel drive carrying it through all theatres of war and over all kinds of ground, including the North African desert where it was used by the machine gunners of the fast-moving raiding parties of the Special Air Service. It also served as a personnel carrier, an ambulance and a gun tractor; it ran on flanged wheels on railway lines and there was even an amphibious version. The name Jeep was, in fact, derived from its army classification, 'GP' for general purpose. A boxy four-seater with a canvas hood, the Jeep was normally equipped with a four-cylinder 2.2 litre engine giving 60 bhp. It was originally built by Willys who, in 1941, won a first order for 16,000. It was so successful Willys was joined by Ford and a total of 639,245 were made before the war ended. The Jeep earned its right to be called a 'performance car' the hard way.

Chrysler Newport

A what-might-have-been-car but for World War Two. This was what the trade calls an 'ideas car', built not for immediate production but to test out designs and obtain public reaction as a guide to tomorrow's cars. Six were built, one of which served as pacemarker for the 1941 Indianapolis 500 mile race; the others were displayed at motor shows. The car had a body built by the coachbuilding firm of LeBaron on the chassis of a Chrysler Imperial. It incorporated dual cockpits with separate folding windshields, a hydraulically controlled disappearing top, push-button door handles and concealed headlamps. The exterior was painted white and the interior trimmed with red leather. But World War Two was about to embroil America as it already had Europe and private car production was to end.

The Postwar Years 1945–1960

After the war production soon returned to normal in America; but in Europe, where there were shortages of raw materials, it took longer. The first cars to go on sale were based on pre-war designs and completely new models were not seen for two or three years. Petrol rationing ended, faster roads were built and there were new customers for cars, some of which were now of unitary construction — without a separate chassis.

There were vogues for open two-seat sports cars and handsome GT cars, and performance was aided by the development of radial-ply tyres and disc brakes. Racing restarted in France in 1945 though Grand Prix events, newly termed Formula One, did not begin until 1947. Supercharging began to be phased out in favour of less-stressed engines, and British cars and drivers gradually began to achieve pre-eminence.

Ferrari 166

"It's small, red and ugly — but it goes like a rocket." That was the verdict of an Italian journalist on the first Ferrari, when Enzo Ferrari moved on from running a stable of racing Alfa Romeos to making and racing cars under his own name. His first big winner, and the first Ferrari to be sold commercially, was the 166 which had a V12 engine of 2 litres behind its bulbous nose. It was capable of 105 mph in its lowest form of tune and 136 mph in its most advanced form, the Mille Miglia version, named for its success in that race, which it won in 1948, 1949 and 1950. This is a 1948 Type 166 Corsa Spyder.

Ferrari 553

Nicknamed the 'Squalo' (shark), this car was built by Ferrari for the new Formula One limit of 2.5 litres unsupercharged, introduced in 1954 by which time supercharging, which placed considerable stress on small engines, had practically been abandoned in favour of simpler, bigger, less-stressed units. It had a four-cylinder engine of 2.5 litres and the blond, bow-tied British driver, Mike Hawthorn, won the Spanish Grand Prix in it at 97.17 mph, ahead of a Maserati and a Mercedes. Hawthorn ended that year third in the drivers' world championship; four years later he won it — in a Ferrari.

Maserati 300S

The Maserati brothers, who founded the family firm, sold out to the Orsi company after the war, but the new owners continued the Maserati tradition of building only racing cars, moving into sports car racing in a major way in the mid-Fifties. Their entry was this handsome car based on the 250F Grand Prix racer, with the six-cylinder engine enlarged to 3 litres, giving 250 bhp. It made its debut in 1955, but though it had some successes it was not equal to the Mercedes, Ferraris and Jaguars. During 1957 the 300S was superseded by a 4.5 litre V8-engined car.

Porsche 356

Ferdinand Porsche had designed cars for Mercedes-Benz and Auto Union, among others, before creating the world-beating Volkswagen, but this two-door coupé, launched in 1950, was the first car to carry his own name. The Type 356 followed Volkswagen practice in having an air-cooled engine in the tail, the original engine being of 1086 cc. The 85 mph car was used in races, sprints, hill climbs and rallies, and scored many victories in the 1100 cc class. Bigger engines of up to 1.6 litres raised the speed to 130 mph and brought class wins in the Mille Miglia of 1957 and the Targa Florio of 1958. Ferdinand Porsche died in 1952 but the firm continued under the direction of his son, Ferry Porsche, establishing a name for small, well-engineered, fast cars.

Fiat V8

The only V8-engined Fiat ever sold to the public, this two-seat coupé was intended for the Italian who hankered for a Ferrari, Alfa Romeo or Maserati, but could not quite afford one of those super-cars. It was a narrow car and consequently the passenger seat was set back behind the position of the driver's by about a foot, to give the driver more elbow room. The 2 litre engine gave it a speed of 120 mph and it won its class in the Italian GT championship of 1954. But it seemed that Fiat had not done sufficient research into the potential market. (Indeed, it was suggested that it had been built by enthusiastic engineers without consulting the sales department.) At any rate, only 114 were sold during its three years in production from 1952 to 1954.

Triumph TR2

This was Triumph's bid to compete with the little sports cars of MG and Morgan, and it did so very successfully. Triumph had been taken over by Standard in 1945 and so it used a Standard Vanguard engine of 2 litres in its own two-seat body. It could reach 110 mph and yet gave 30 miles per gallon. It was a good rally car, winning the RAC rally in 1954, and also a useful club racer. It was succeeded by the TR3 in 1955 and then by the TR3A, which was to be the most popular British rally car of the Fifties. The TR range continued to the TR8, production of which finally ceased in 1981.

Sunbeam Alpine

The Rootes Group's contender in the open two-seat sports car market in 1953 was the Sunbeam Alpine, a modified 100 mph version of the 77 mph Sunbeam-Talbot 90 saloon, with a 2.3 litre engine. A stripped-down model was driven at 120 mph near Ostend by Sheila Van Damm, who joined Stirling Moss in winning cups at the wheel of Alpines in — appropriately — the Alpine Rally of 1954. But the car was heavy, a legacy of its saloon car parentage, and it was discontinued in 1955. The name was, however, revived in 1960 for a 1.5 litre 98 mph tourer with the tail fins that were in style at that time. That series continued until 1968. Here the 1953 Alpine is seen capturing the one-hour record at Montlhery with a distance of 111.20 miles.

Frazer Nash Le Mans

The name of Frazer Nash cars (spelt without a hyphen) built by Archie Frazer-Nash (with a hyphen) had been established in the Twenties and Thirties by a succession of chain-driven two-seaters, every one of which was used in competitions such as hill climbs and trials. In 1948 came the High Speed model with a Bristol 2 litre engine based on that of the pre-war BMW, and a year later, in the first postwar Le Mans race, a car driven by Norman Culpan and H. J. Aldington (by then the head of Frazer Nash) took third place. After this it was renamed the Le Mans Replica. Franco Cortese won the 1951 Targa Florio in one — the only British car to win the event — but only 105 Frazer Nashes were built in the postwar years. Beset by financial problems the company withdrew from racing in 1955 and ceased production in 1960.

Healey Silverstone

Donald Healey, formerly technical director of Triumph, began making his own cars in 1946, and the most famous of them was the 1950 Silverstone model, a two-seater with cycle type wings, propelled by a four-cylinder 2.4 litre Riley engine. Unusual features were the tail-mounted spare tyre, which also acted as a bumper, and, on some cars, the headlamps mounted behind the radiator grille. However, Healey's production was always small and ended completely in 1954, after it had been taken over by the British Motor Corporation, subsequent cars being known as Austin-Healeys.

Austin-Healey 100

Austin's involvement in this car was noteworthy; it was practically the first time a British mass-production company had taken an interest in small sports cars. Austin were rewarded. Healey designed the car, launched in 1952, to use as many stock BMC components as possible, including a four-cylinder 2.6 litre Austin engine, and it became a major rival to the Triumph TR and highly popular in the United States. It had a speed of 105 mph, with the disc-braked 100S version running up to 120 mph. In 1953 one averaged 123 mph over 12 hours. Production of the original four-cylinder engine ended in 1956, after which the car had a six-cylinder unit of the same capacity, bored out to 2.9 litres in 1959 when the car was renamed the Austin-Healey 3000. By that time it was widely known as 'the big Healey' to distinguish it from the Austin-Healey Sprite, launched in 1958 with a 948 cc engine.

MGA

The TR2 and Austin-Healey cars made the MG Midget appear dated. MG's reply was the MGA, a 1.5 litre car more comfortable and refined than the Midget, yet still with near 100 mph performance. Launched in 1956, it brought new honour to the name. The Twin Cam, a twin overhead camshaft version with a four-cylinder 1.6 litre engine, introduced in 1958 in both open roadster and coupé form, was capable of 115 mph, and the same engine powered the record-breaking EX181 to 250 mph in Utah in 1959. Unfortunately, the Twin Cam achieved a name for unreliability. It still sold around 2,000 out of a total of 100,000 MGAs during seven years, by which time it had been superseded by the MGB with a 1.8 litre engine.

Lotus 7

Colin Chapman, seen here with his Lotus 7, began his career by building specials, trials cars based on Austin Sevens, and these led to the foundation of Lotus in 1952. There followed a range of small, sporty cars, the most famous of which remains the Mark 7, with a Ford engine of 1172 cc. It was sold in kit form so that do-it-yourself enthusiasts could assemble it at home, avoiding British purchase tax. It triggered a boom in kit cars, mostly with glass fibre bodies, as had later versions of the Lotus. The car was primitive but fast (particularly in the Super Seven version powered by a Coventry-Climax engine). It was featured by Patrick McGoohan in his cult TV series *The Prisoner* and some 2,700 were sold before it ceased production in the Seventies.

Lotus F1

Colin Chapman was a genius at engineering fast cars and was to have a major influence on the design of Grand Prix racers. He moved on from sports racing cars to F2 in 1957 and F1 in 1958. The car above was his first Grand Prix model, equipped with a four-cylinder Coventry-Climax engine of 1.5 litres for F2 races and 2.5 for F1. Graham Hill equalled the Monza lap record in it during practice for the 1959 Italian GP; but although it was fast it was not as reliable as the Coopers using the same engine, and Lotus had to wait for its first success until 1960 when Stirling Moss, in a privately entered car, won at Monaco. After that development was rapid.

Lotus Elite

This two-seat coupé was the first true road car to wear the Lotus badge. It was also the first production car to combine a glass fibre body and unitary construction — without a separate chassis. Extremely light as a result, and with all-independent springing, it had a Coventry-Climax engine of 1.2 litres and could reach 113 mph. It won class victories at Le Mans in 1959, 1960, 1962, 1963 and 1964, and had many successes in club races. It was sold both in assembled and kit form and more than a thousand were built between 1959, when full production began, and 1963 when, because of the cost of the glass fibre unitary bodies, Lotus moved on to the Elan with a steel chassis.

Aston Martin DB2/4

'DB' were the initials of industrialist David Brown, who acquired the company in 1947. The DB1 was a 2 litre car in 1948, followed in 1950 by the DB2, which combined an Aston Martin chassis with a six-cylinder 2.6 litre Lagonda engine (Brown had also acquired Lagonda). Its two-door bodywork was by Tickford, also owned by the same parent company. The DB2 could pass 100 mph effortlessly and the car did well at Le Mans in 1950 and 1951. The DB2/4, which followed in 1953, had a 2.9 litre engine and so-called occasional seats in the back for children or small adults, an early version of what came to be called 2 + 2 seating. The car led in 1957 to the DB3, a sports racer.

Mercedes-Benz 300SL

Its gull-wing doors, hinged on the top edge and opening upwards, made this one of the most distinctive cars ever built. They resulted from the use of a multi-tubular spaceframe. A sports racing car with a six-cylinder 3 litre engine and direct fuel injection, it had a top speed of around 130 mph when geared for British sales and roads; in its most highly tuned form was capable of about 165 mph. Although a prototype ran at Le Mans — and won — in 1952, full production did not begin until 1955, after which some 1,400 were built before 1963.

Jaguar XK 140

Undoubtedly the most exciting British car of the immediate postwar period was the Jaguar XK 120 announced in 1948. Its six-cylinder 3.4 litre engine had been designed to power the forthcoming Mark 7 saloon, but William Lyons thought there was publicity to be won by putting it in 200 two-seat sports cars. The car's title indicated an advertised speed of 120 mph but it was faster than this, even in normal roadgoing trim, and in 1949 one covered a flying mile in Belgium at 132.4 mph. It eventually sold 12,000, all but 2,000 of which went for export. It led in 1954 to the XK 140, with better steering and more power, of which 9,000 were sold, and in 1957 to the XK 150, with still more power and four-wheel disc brakes, of which 9,500 were made. They were great rally cars and useful racers, while the engine also powered saloons, ambulances and armoured cars. Production of the XKs ended in 1961 with the introduction of the E-Type Jaguar.

Jaguar D-Type

The Jaguar XK 120, though not designed for racing, was competing at Le Mans in 1950 and the engine was so good it led to the Jaguar C-Type, a 150 mph disc-braked version built purely to win Le Mans, which it did in 1951 and 1952. The car had beautiful rounded lines, designed by Malcolm Sayer with the aid of a wind tunnel, and 50 were built before it was followed in 1954 by the D-Type, with the same six-cylinder 3.4 litre engine but capable of 180 mph. This two-seater, without any hood and with only a shallow wraparound windscreen, won in 1955, 1956 and 1957, equalling the record of the great Bentleys of the Twenties. In addition to 17 works cars, 42 were built for sale and there were also 16 XK SS cars, with hoods and passenger doors, for use on the road.

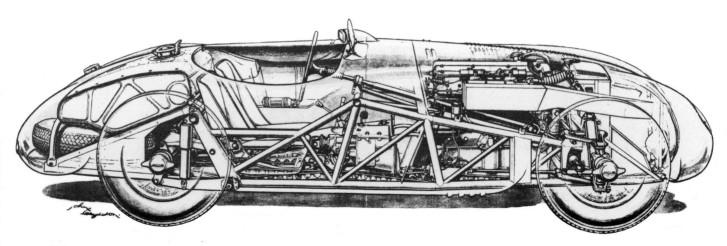

BRM V16

Raymond Mays and Peter Berthon, who created the pre-war ERA voiturette, dreamed of a British Grand Prix winner, and the result of their dream was the BRM (British Racing Motor), backed by a number of British companies and even the pennies of patriotic members of the public. With the F1 formula calling for cars below 4.5 litres unsupercharged or 1.5 litres blown, they created a supercharged V16 1.5 litre car, the most advanced and powerful of its day. It was capable of 190 mph and the shrill scream of its engine, generating 450 bhp at 12,000 rpm, excited all who heard it. But when it came to its debut in 1950 and Raymond Sommer let in the clutch the transmission failed and it had to be pushed ignominiously away. More humiliations followed; the potential was always there but the car was over-sophisticated, and with a new 2.5 litre formula scheduled for 1954, and with supercharging effectively dead, it became apparent that the car could never be got right in time.

Vanwall Special

Tony Vandervell, millionaire head of a bearings company, was one of the original backers of the BRM, but withdrew in 1951 after differences with other sponsors, and started his own racing stable, running at first with a modified 4.5 litre Ferrari named the *Thinwall Special*. This was followed in 1955 by the Vanwall Special with a 2.3 litre (later 2.5) engine, driven by Mike Hawthorn (seen here). In the following year it was given a new body and chassis, and Stirling Moss piloted it to its first victories. Though Mike Hawthorn won the Drivers' World Championship in a Ferrari, the Constructors' Championship went to Vanwall as the result of wins by Stirling Moss and Tony Brooks.

Maserati 250F

One of the last great conventional front-engined racing cars, the six-cylinder Maserati 250F was built for the 2.5 litre unsupercharged Grand Prix formula introduced in 1954. The 170 mph car designed by Vittorio Colombo was built not merely for the works team but also for sale to private entrants; 32 were made, and 12 of them were on the starting grid for one race. The car won the first race in which it competed, the 1954 Argentine Grand Prix, when it was driven by Juan Manuel Fangio.

Ford Thunderbird

British sports cars enjoyed enormous popularity in America in the late Forties and early Fifties, for no equivalent cars were made in volume in the United States. However, in 1955 Ford introduced the 112 mph Thunderbird which became the dream of every young American male, selling 53,000 in its first three years. It was a low two-seater with a folding hood or detachable hardtop, and its spare wheel was placed on the back bumper in imitation of European practice. The engine was originally a V8 of 4.8 litres, later increased to 5.1 litres, but in 1958 the car was enlarged to family-seating size, and much of its glamour and appeal faded.

Renault Etoile Filante

The first gas-turbine engined car, Rover's aptly registered JET 1, was demonstrated in 1950, and was basically a Rover 75 with a sports body, which reached 150 mph in test runs. Other manufacturers began experiments with gas turbines, among them Fiat in Italy, General Motors in America and Renault in France. The Etoile Filante (Shooting Star) was built in 1956 and, driven by J. Hebert, it reached 191.2 mph over a one-mile course from a flying start. But it was never raced or put into production; the problems with gas turbines, as Rover had discovered, were high costs and a high level of fuel consumption, and also a lag in throttle response.

Bristol 404

Among the most stylish cars of the immediate postwar period was the Bristol, built by the Bristol Aeroplane Company and as aerodynamic as one might expect from such a firm. They branched into cars in 1947, using the designs of pre-war BMW cars and the BMW 328 engine.

The original Bristol 400, a six-cylinder 2 litre car, capable of 90 to 95 mph, was third in the Monte Carlo Rally and also the Mille Miglia of 1949. It led in 1950 to the 401 and in 1958 to the 404, with steadily improving performance. The 404, known as the 'Businessman's Express' was a closed car, basically a two-seater but with extra room for a child or dog. It was capable of 110 mph, and was a good rally car.

Lancia Aurelia

This is the car that has been credited with starting the GT fashion, the letters standing for 'gran turismo' or 'grand touring' and meaning a comfortable, high-performance tourer. When it was introduced in 1950 it had a V6 engine of 1.7 litres, increased within a year to 2 litres which gave a speed of 100 mph. Then it grew to 2.4 litres and the speed rose to 112 mph. It had the gear change on the steering column, but that was the vogue at the time. Nevertheless it won the Targa Florio and the Liege-Rome-Liege in 1953, the Monte Carlo Rally in 1954 and the Acropolis Rally in 1958.

Rolls-Royce Silver Dawn

This was a new departure for Rolls-Royce, a factory-bodied model. Until this time the bodywork of a Rolls had been supplied by various coachbuilding concerns to the customer's choice, but this car was intended for export, particularly to America, hence the standard bodywork, and also left-hand drive and steering column gearchange. When introduced in 1949 it had a six-cylinder 4.2 litre engine but this was increased during the Fifties to 4.6 litres and then 4.9 litres, and the car was made available with General Motors Hydramatic auto-transmission. The car led in 1955 to the Silver Cloud.

Bentley Continental

One of the few distinctive Bentleys to be produced after the company merged with Rolls-Royce and models became practically the same, the Continental was the fastest four-seater of its day. Introduced in 1952 with a six-cylinder 4.5 litre engine, it could cruise at close on 100 mph and had a top speed of 120 mph. The most often seen body was a two-door fastback style by Mulliner. The car was given a 4.9 litre engine and an automatic gearbox in 1955, power-assisted steering and air conditioning in 1957, and a V8 engine of 6.2 litres in 1960. It was not cheap, £7,000 when launched, but it was a classic car.

Performers of the Sixties 1961–1970

Following wars in the Middle East (which sent the price rocketing) there was a campaign to save petrol, and concern about the rate at which the world's oil reserves were being used. A campaign was mounted, mainly in America, against pollution by exhaust emissions. There was also a campaign for safer cars, which led to the compulsory fitting of seat belts, stronger seat anchorage, energy-absorbing steering columns, head restraints, warning flashers and more. These campaigns, combined with the imposition of blanket speed limits — 70 mph in Britain — tended to curb the performance of cars. Yet, at the same time, cars became more efficient, particularly small cars such as the BMC Mini, the model which led to widespread adoption of front-wheel drive. In racing most cars came to be powered by the same engines and to look alike, though they became more colourful as constructors, desperately seeking sponsorship to offset mounting costs, turned them into high-speed advertising sites.

Chevrolet Corvair Monza Convertible

As the Fifties turned to the Sixties the Americans turned to smaller and less thirsty cars — the so-called 'compacts', though they were compact only by traditional American standards. The Corvair had a rear-mounted and air-cooled six-cylinder engine of 2.3 litres and was of unitary construction, which was new in the United States. It became one of the country's favourite rally cars, winning the national rally championship in 1967, and 1.4 million were sold. But it had vices such as oversteering and brakes which some thought inadequate. Ralph Nader, the lawyer who led the consumer movement and campaigned for improved safety features in cars, singled it out for particular attack in the mid-Sixties and it was phased out in 1969.

Ford Falcon

Ford's compact for 1960 was the 15 ft. 1 in. long Falcon, produced in a range of two- and four-door sedans and station wagons with a six-cylinder 2.3 litre engine. Two years later Ford began using it extensively in competitions (along with 7 litre Galaxies and Cobras) and a team of Falcon Sprints including the one pictured dominated its class in the 1963 Monte Carlo Rally. The car was also successful in saloon car races and Britain's Mike Hawthorn was among its drivers.

Ford Mustang

Introduced in 1963, the Mustang was based on the Falcon and used many of its components, but it was aimed from the start at the sporting drivers, who had complained that the Thunderbird had became staid. It typified motor marketing in the Sixties, being available in a range of packages or options. It could be had with a straight-six cylinder or V8 engine, in sizes ranging from 2.8 litres to 4.7 litres, with power output from 101 bhp to 270 bhp and with a top speed of 95 mph to 118 mph. There was also a Carroll Shelby-tuned Mustang GT350, delivering 350 bhp from a 4.7 litre engine, which could hit 130 mph even as a road car.

Ford GT40

Ford embarked on a worldwide campaign to improve its image by building race-winning cars and engines, the first phase being an assault on the Le Mans 24 hours race, then dominated by Ferrari mid-engined cars. Ford's weapon was the GT40, so called because it was just 40 inches high. It was a mid-engined car with a V8 engine of 4.2 litres and a top speed of 200 mph, but its debut at Le Mans in 1964 was a flop; Ferraris finished first, second and third, and the same thing happened in 1965. Then in 1966 came the Mark 2 car pictured, with a 7 litre engine giving 400 bhp; Bruce McLaren and Chris Amon drove it to victory with other GT40s second and third. The car won again in 1967, 1968 and 1969.

BRM V8

After the failure of the original BRM V16, the BRM concern was put on the market and bought by the Owen group of companies, but the marque was little more successful during the 2.5 litre Formula One of the late Fifties. Then in 1961 came a 1.5 litre for which BRM built a V8-engined car and all was changed; in 1962 Graham Hill, after a season-long battle with Jim Clark, driving for Lotus, won four *grandes epreuves*, securing the drivers' world championship for himself and the constructors' championship for BRM. Hill and BRM came second in 1963, 1964 and 1965.

Rover Gas Turbines

Rover continued the experiments with gas-turbine engined cars it had begun in 1950, and in 1963 joined forces with BRM to produce this two-seat racer in which Graham Hill and Richie Ginther averaged 107.84 mph over 24 hours in a demonstration at Le Mans. If it had been competing that performance would have given it seventh place. However, when a rebodied car with two heat exchangers to pre-heat ingoing air competed in the 1965 race, driven by Hill and Jackie Stewart, it could average only 98.2 mph and finished tenth. Development was then abandoned, although other companies continued experiments. The picture shows four generations of Rover gas-turbine cars: JET 1, the original 1950 car; T3, a rear-engined four-wheel-drive car built in 1956; T4, a front-wheel-drive car built in 1961, and the Rover-BRM with Hill at the wheel.

Lotus-Climax V8

The Formula One Lotus of 1962–3 changed the look of Grand Prix cars. To save weight in the 1.5 litre formula, Colin Chapman went over to monocoque construction using a chassis-less shell in place of the normal multi-tubular spaceframe. Most other constructors were soon using the same Coventry-Climax V8 engine in similar monocoques; soon the cars were lapping faster than 2.5 litre cars of a few years earlier. Clark won the world championship with Lotus in 1963 and again in 1965.

Brabham-Repco BT24

When the 3 litre Formula One began in 1966 most manufacturers built new V12 engines and suffered the inevitable early teething troubles. Australia's Jack Brabham, who had been world champion in 1959 and 1960 in Cooper-Climax cars, before starting to build his own cars, decided that reliability was more important than power at this time and settled for the Repco V8 engine, built for him by an Australian team headed by Phil Irving, and based on a discontinued 3.5 litre General Motors engine block. With 330 bhp at 8,800 rpm it was underpowered but absolutely reliable. It kept on going when more sophisticated machines stopped and 1966 ended with Brabham the first driver to win the world championship in a car of his own make. The following year his team leader, New Zealander Denny Hulme, won the title with Brabham second, but by then other constructors had got their V12s sorted out and the Repco was outclassed.

Lola T70

After seeing the Ford GT40 launched, Eric Broadley turned his attention to the creation of more Lolas, among them the Mark Two T70 of 1966 in which John Surtees won that year's Canadian American (Can-Am) Championship with three first places. Its glass fibre body housed a Chevrolet V8 engine of 5 litres, delivering 430 bhp at 6,000 rpm. The car was used by a number of racing teams against works cars in sports car races, particularly long-distance events, and other noted drivers included Denny Hulme, Frank Gardner and Chris Craft.

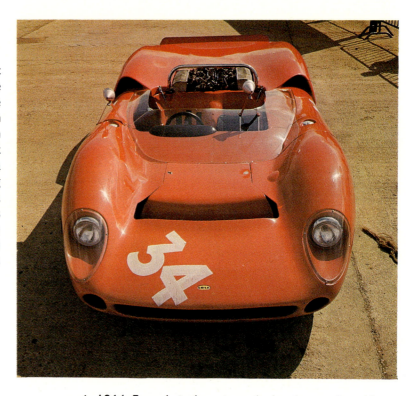

AC Cobra

Texan racing driver Carroll Shelby created the Cobra by shipping AC Ace bodies from the Thames Ditton firm to California and there installing in them Ford V8 engines and transmissions. The first cars in 1962 had 4.2 litre engines, but from 1963 he used 4.7 litre engines as in the model pictured, which won the world GT championship in 1964. For sale in America only, he also produced from 1965 7 litre cars with wider wheels and tyres. Acceleration of the 4.7 litre was spectacular with 0–60 in 5.5 seconds and a top speed of 138 mph, while the 7 litre's performance was breathtaking. It had a top speed of 195 mph and could go from 0 to 100 and back to rest — twice — within 30 seconds! Production of the cars, known variously as AC Cobras, Shelby Cobras and Ford Cobras, ended in 1968.

McLaren M8B

McLaren cars won the Can-Am series four times in a row between 1967 and 1969, the M8B being the 1969 car with a Chevrolet V8 engine of 7 litres developing 625 bhp at 7,000 rpm. It could reach 100 mph in less than six seconds and top 200 mph. Bruce McLaren himself and his fellow New Zealander Denny Hulme were the main drivers, completely dominating the Can-Am series, and McLaren won the championship. He was killed in 1970 testing his M8D Can-Am car at Goodwood, before he could receive the Segrave Trophy, awarded to him for his achievements as driver and constructor.

Chevron B8

Motor racing, despite rising cost, continued to be a sport in which small specialist constructors could compete successfully against the giants. Such a firm was Chevron, founded by Derek Bennett, a driver who had built his first car — based on an Austin 7 — at the age of 19 in 1954. In 1965 he built two Ford-engined sports cars for clubman races, one for his own use and one for a friend, and they were practically unbeatable. Bennett then set up his own company, operating from a mill in Bolton. His B8 of 1968 was a production version of a GT car raced by the Chevron team. Most of those built had BMW 2 litre engines, though some ran with Coventry-Climax and Cosworth FVA 2 litre units.

BMC Mini

Created by Alec (later Sir Alec) Issigonis, who had designed the Morris Minor a decade earlier, the Mini-Minor, as it was originally known in 1960, brought a revolution in motoring. A boxy little car, 10 ft. long, it was new in almost every way, with the front wheels driven by a four-cylinder 848 cc water-cooled engine placed transversely in its snub nose to save space. The suspension, developed by Alex Moulton, who had already re-thought bicycle design, used rubber cone springs, later superseded by the Hydrolastic system of interconnecting pipes containing a mixture of alcohol and water. An economical runabout with a speed of 69 mph in its original Austin and Morris form (only the radiator grilles were different) it also had incredible roadholding and there were soon hotted-up 100 mph Cooper variants with twin carburettor engines of up to 1.3 litres, the result of collaboration with John Cooper's racing firm. Paddy Hopkirk and Henry Liddon drove one to victory in the Monte Carlo rally of 1964, the first of a hat-trick of Mini wins in that event; the Mini was also much used in saloon car racing. A million had been made by 1965, four million by 1977 and the classless Mini goes on.

Ford Cortina GT

The Consul Cortina, as it was originally known, was launched in 1962 as a strictly basic no-nonsense car for the company salesman and the family man of modest income, the Mark I version having a 1.2 litre engine and a top speed of 78 mph, but the car was so popular that performance versions were inevitable. When the Mark 2 followed in 1966 there was a range of engine options, including a 1.6 litre Cortina GT for the man who wanted extra dash, and it was much used in rallies and club competitions. There was also a Cortina Lotus, the result of an association with Colin Chapman's firm. The Mark 2 continued until 1970, establishing the Cortina as Britain's biggest-selling car. Marks 3 and 4 followed and the name Cortina was dropped only in 1982 after 4.3 million had been sold, when the Sierra was launched.

MGB

The successor to the MGA in 1962 was an open two-seater with a 1.8 litre engine, followed in 1965 by the MGB GT, a fixed-roof coupé, and this was destined to be the most successful of postwar MGs. Like earlier models it was a favourite in America, until its looks were marred by impact-absorbing bumpers which American safety regulations required to be fixed at a mandatory height, and its performance was curbed by equally compulsory smog-emission control devices. Nevertheless, it continued to be built until 1980 when all MG production was ended by the parent company, British Leyland.

Jaguar E-Type

The favourite sports car of the Sixties, the E-Type, replaced the XK 150 in 1961, retaining its six-cylinder 3.8 litre engine, though its lines owed more to the racing D-Type. It could reach 150 mph, with 100 mph coming up from rest in 16 seconds; it had all-independent suspension and disc brakes all round. Yet the price tag was £2,200, compared with around £6,000 for the commonest Ferrari. In 1965 its engine was enlarged to 4.2 litres and in 1970 it acquired a V12 engine of 5.3 litres, along with fatter wheels and tyres. By this time the original open and closed two-seaters had been joined by a 2 + 2 coupé body. The E-Type continued in production until 1974, by which time sales totalled 72,584, of which more than 49,000 were in the United States.

De Tomaso Vallelunga

Alessandro de Tomaso was an Argentinian racing driver who began building his own cars in Italy in the early Sixties, the first being the mid-engined Vallelunga GT coupé, named after the race circuit near Rome. The first 50 cars were equipped with a 1.5 litre Ford Cortina engine, but this was replaced by the 4.7 litre Ford V8 engine used in the Shelby Cobra. The Vallelunga was followed by other sleek, powerful and expensive machines, and de Tomaso also acquired the coachbuilding firm of Ghia in the Sixties, and Maserati in the Seventies.

Ferrari 246 GT Dino

This was the first mid-engined Ferrari road car, which came about in 1967 because of Enzo Ferrari's desire to race in the Formula Two category in which the rules stipulated production-based engines. So a deal was made with Fiat for volume production and the engine was put into this car, the name Dino being in memory of Enzo's son Alfredino, who had worked on the engine's development before he died, a victim of muscular dystrophy, in 1956. The engine, mounted transversely behind the seats, was a V6 of 2.4 litres giving the car a speed of 140 mph. It was superseded in 1974 by the 308 GTB with a V8 engine.

Reliant Scimitar

Previously best-known for small three-wheelers, Reliant made its first sports car, the Sabre, in 1962, and this led in 1966 to the Scimitar GT, a stylish coupé with a six-cylinder Ford Zephyr engine of 2.5 litres. Three years later the firm introduced what it called a station wagon version of the coupé, seen in the picture. It was, in fact, an early form of what was to become known as a hatchback. A 100 mph load-carrier was obviously what many had been waiting for — among them members of the British royal family who used one extensively when off duty, and this version was so popular that the coupé was phased out in its favour in 1970.

Range Rover

America's Jeep was the inspiration for Britain's postwar Land Rover, launched in 1949 with a 2.2 litre engine and four-wheel drive, and used for innumerable purposes. Many wanted something more, and this arrived in 1970 in the Range Rover, a bigger four-wheel-drive, go-anywhere vehicle, more car than truck, and a luxury car at that, with deep carpets and wood door capping. Its V8 engine of 3.5 litres gave it a speed of 100 mph and it became standard equipment for expeditions to every part of the world, carrying large loads over rough country at speed. It was also adopted by police for motorway patrol duties. Many imitations have since been produced, particularly in Japan.

Mercedes-Benz C111

The rotary engine, developed by Germany's Felix Wankel, was the most promising new kind of engine in the Sixties, and Mercedes-Benz built this research and development car to test it at high speed. The first model in 1969 used a triple rotor engine, comparable to a conventional engine of 3.6 litres, which was placed behind the two seats in the glass fibre-reinforced synthetic body, and with direct fuel injection it gave 330 bhp at 7,000 rpm. Five seconds took the car from 0 to 62 mph and it could go on to reach 162 mph. A four-rotor engine installed in 1970 increased the power to 350 bhp and top speed to 190 mph, but problems remained with the engines, the most powerful and sophisticated rotaries ever built, and the car remained an 'ideas car'.

Volvo P1800

Still identified by some television viewers as the car used by Roger Moore in the series *The Saint*, in which he starred as the Leslie Charteris hero, the Volvo P1800 two-seater sports coupé was introduced in 1960. Because Volvo was short of factory space it was for a time assembled in Birmingham, the body shells being made in Britain and the four-cylinder 1.8 litre engines and other components in Sweden. Later Volvo assembled the complete cars in Sweden, those cars being termed the P1800S, with the suffix letter standing for the country. In 1967 petrol injection was introduced and in 1968 a 2 litre engine, but production ended in 1973. It was Volvo's last sports car; the name has since been associated with weighty 'safety' saloons.

Saab 96

The Swedish aircraft company began manufacturing cars after World War Two and their little two-strokes were made famous by the rally successes of a big Swedish driver named Eric Carlsson. He became the first rally driver to achieve the same kind of fame as Grand Prix champions when he won the RAC Rally of 1960 in a Saab saloon with an 841 cc engine. He went on to win the RAC Rally for three years in succession. He also won the Monte Carlo Rally twice running — in 1962 and 1963. It was not until 1967 that Saab abandoned its two-stroke engines in favour of a four-stroke, when the car was given a V4 of 1.5 litres with which it continued until the end of the Seventies.

Alpine Renault A110 Berlinette

The Alpine firm was founded in Dieppe by Jean Redele, a Renault dealer, and its first car was a glass fibre coupé based on a Renault 750. Subsequent cars based on the Renault Dauphine were raced and rallied extensively. Rally cars need to be strong and the A110, with a 1.8 litre engine delivering 200 bhp, was exceptionally strong and became an international rally winner. In 1969, when the company became effectively the competition arm of Renault, it withdrew from racing to concentrate on rallies (it is seen here during the 1970 Monte Carlo Rally), winning the Acropolis and the Italian in that year. In 1973 it won the world rally championships. The A110 continued until 1977 when it was replaced by the A310.

Porsche 911S

To replace the Porsche 356 the 911 went into production in 1965. It had a rear-mounted, air-cooled flat-six engine of 2 litres, and the tuned 911S version used in races and rallies was capable of 130 mph. This gave Porsche its first success in the Monte Carlo Rally. Until 1967 the handicapping was not favourable to GT cars, but then the handicapping was scrapped and Vic Elford won the rally in 1968, Bjorn Waldegaard in 1969 and 1970. By this time the engine had been increased in size to 2.2 litres.

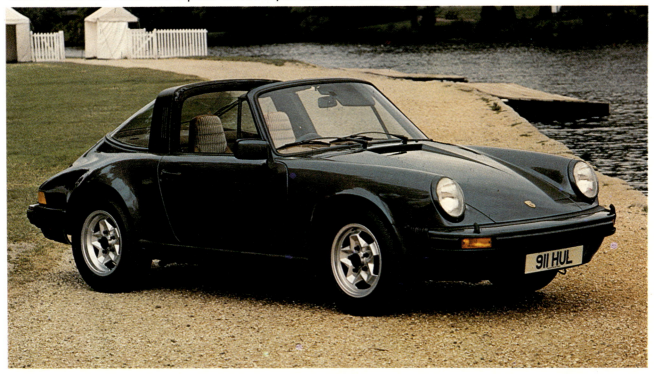

Bluebird

Sir Malcolm Campbell had died in 1948 but his son Donald was equally obsessed with speed and took up the pursuit of the world land speed record set at 394.20 mph by John Cobb in 1957. His car was named Bluebird as his father's had been, though Donald's was powered by a Proteus aircraft turbine engine and cost around £1 million. In 1964, on the bed of dried up Lake Eyre in Australia, Campbell pushed up the record to 403.01 mph. In fact, this speed had already been exceeded by Craig Breedlove, an American, in his Spirit of America, but it was not recognised as a world record because his vehicle was a three-wheeler, which was classed as a motorcycle, and because it was jet-propelled and not driven through the wheels in the conventional way.

Spirit of America — Sonic 1

From November 1964 the rules governing the world land speed record were amended to make any vehicle eligible provided it had a driver and it depended on the ground for support. This made jets acceptable and a duel began between Craig Breedlove and Art Arfons, another American, both driving cars powered by General Electric turbojets. In 1965, in his four-wheeled Spirit of America — Sonic 1, Breedlove became the first man to exceed 600 mph when his aluminium and glass fibre capsule sped across Bonneville Salt Flats at an average of 600.601 mph. Campbell had by this time switched to pursuit of the world water speed record in the course of which in 1967 he died as Segrave and Cobb had done before him.

Blue Flame

The jet age in record breaking led quickly to the rocket age. Gary Gabelich, an American who had trained as an astronaut, went after Breedlove's record in a car with an engine similar to those used in the space programme. Fuelled by liquefied natural gas and hydrogen peroxide, it was installed in the longest-ever record car — 38 ft. 2½ in. long, and with a tail fin ending 8 ft. 1½ in. above the ground, and parachutes to provide the ultimate braking power. It was a four-wheeler, although the two front wheels were so close set they looked like one. In a yellow T shirt and a black stocking cap, wearing 28 strings of beads and a St. Christopher medal, Gabelich took the record to 622.407 mph in 1970. Drivers began to talk about the 1,000 mph barrier, but there was no longer much connection with motoring.

Today . . . and Tomorrow

The Japanese, who had only a small motor industry before World War Two, outstripped even the Americans in the Seventies to become the world's biggest manufacturers and also the world's biggest exporters of cars. The turbocharger, a form of supercharger driven by exhaust gases rather than mechanical means, became popular not merely to increase power but to improve torque at low engine speeds, while diesel engines, though far from new, gained new acceptance because of the lower cost of diesel fuel. Designers concentrated on reducing drag to improve performance and save fuel, and electronics came to cars. In motor racing the 3 litre Formula One continued into the Eighties, the longest lived and most successful formula of all time, though the same engine, the Ford Cosworth V8, powered all but a few cars.

Lamborghini Countach

Ferruccio Lamborghini manufactured tractors in Italy until — according to popular mythology — he was kept waiting by Enzo Ferrari when he went to buy a Ferrari and was so piqued he decided to make his own, even faster and more striking cars. The Countach, announced in 1971, was a two-seater with a wedge-front, designed by Bertone, with doors opening upwards and forwards. It also had pop-up headlamps and air intakes in the flanks for the midships engine, which was a V12 of 4.7 litres with six twin-choke carburettors giving 375 bhp at 8,000 rpm. The car could accelerate from 0 to 60 mph in 5.6 seconds and on to 165 mph — or more than 180 mph in tuned versions. 'Countach' is a Piedmontese word expressing astonishment and admiration and the car justified the name.

Alfa Romeo Montreal

Italy continued to produce some of the world's fastest and most desirable cars. The somewhat unlikely name of this one came about because it was first displayed as a styling exercise at a show in Montreal in 1967, though it did not go into production until 1970, when it was the fastest Alfa roadster ever built, with a speed of between 130 and 140 mph. This came from a fuel-injected V8 engine of 2.6 litres, a detuned and developed version of the engine that powered the Type 33 racing sports car of the late Sixties. It was installed in a two-door coupé by Bertone with distinctive slatted covers over the headlamps, continuing in production until 1976.

Maserati Ghibli Spyder

It has been called the most beautiful front-engined car ever built, a 2+2 closed coupé styled by Giorgetto Giugiaro. That is something enthusiasts can argue about, but it certainly was handsome and fast, with a top speed of 170 mph from a V8 engine of 4.9 litres developing 330 bhp. Maserati had been a racing organisation before World War Two but had not made a true roadster until 1963; its cars were expensive and never made in large quantities. Just 2,400 examples of the Ghibli were built between 1967 and 1972 (the picture showing a 1970 model), during which time the firm was controlled by Citroën, but the French company's involvement ended in 1973.

Maserati Bora

In 1971 Maserati introduced the Giugiaro-styled Bora and Merak. They looked alike, but the Bora was a two-seater with a V8 engine of 4.7 litres, developed from one used in the company's two-seater racers, while the Merak squeezed in two more small seats, and had a V6 engine of 3 litres, also used in the Citroën SM coupé. The Bora could reach 160 mph on the road, the Merak a mere 140 mph. The air-conditioned, mid-engined cars were in production for only two years when Citröen pulled out of the company and the Maserati lines ground to a halt. However, after a two-year gap, Alessandro de Tomaso took over the firm, and the Bora returned with a 5 litre engine.

Lancia Stratos

In 1973 the Lancia company decided to win publicity in motor sport, particularly rallies. It had been taken over in 1969 by Fiat, which also controlled Ferrari, so it was able to obtain the V6 Ferrari Dino 2.4 litre engine which developed 190 bhp (240 bhp in works cars). Lancia put the engine into a strong, stubby body of its own make, and proceeded to build the 400 cars necessary to qualify for entry in group four (GT) events. In the years that followed the Stratos won almost everything for which it was entered, including production car races and rallies, scoring no fewer than four Monte Carlo victories, and though production ended in 1975 it went on winning for some years afterwards. Rarities were the few cars used on the roads by wealthy enthusiasts.

Panther De Ville

Nostalgia grows for cars of the past, and there are customers for replicas of Cords and Duesenbergs and SS100s. Panther, which was founded by Bob Jankel in the garage of his home at Weybridge in 1971 (later moving into the former factory of the Cooper racing team), specialises not in exact replicas of cars but ones suggesting great marques of bygone days, the De Ville being inspired by Bugatti's famous Royale of the early Thirties. Introduced in 1974 it had a V12 Jaguar engine of 5.3 litres and could reach 128 mph. It had electric windows and a sliding roof, while a cocktail cabinet and TV set could be supplied to order. It was strictly a limited edition, costing as much as a Rolls.

Chevrolet Corvette

The Corvette name was introduced in 1953 when it was attached to the first glass fibre bodied car to be produced in quantity. The car's appearance changed as the years passed, becoming more 'Europeanised'; it could also house a number of alternative engines, but it remained America's only home-grown two-seat sports coupé for most of its life, and was a big seller all the time. The picture shows the 1979 model, when the standard engine was an eight-cylinder of 5.7 litres driving the rear wheels and giving a top speed of 118 mph. A high-compression version of the same engine was also available, and with that the car was capable of 130 mph.

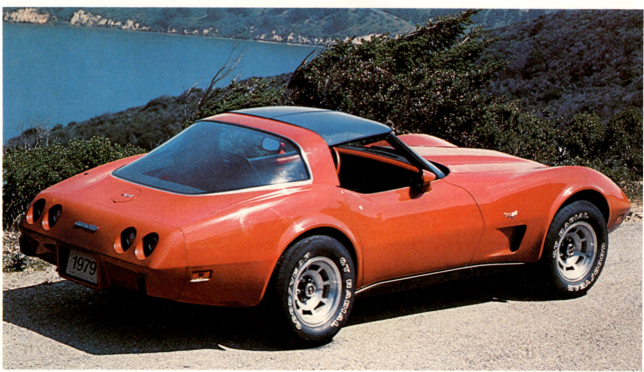

Chrysler Newport

More typically American in appearance was this four-door hardtop, also of 1979. It was more than 18 ft. long and seated up to six people, retaining a bench front seat, albeit with built-in headrests. It was available with a six-cylinder engine of 3.7 litres which gave it a speed of 93 mph, or an eight-cylinder engine of 6 litres which would take it to 106 mph. The smaller engine drank petrol at the rate of 20 mph, the larger one at around 15 mpg. These figures were better than average, for in the mid-Seventies the average American car gave only 12 miles per gallon, but by 1979 the American government had ordered its manufacturers to increase efficiency and set a target of 27.5 mpg.

Dodge Omni 024

A new style of American car was typified by the Dodge Omni (a name inspired by the film *Star Wars*) which was introduced in 1979. This was an American version of Europe's front-wheel-drive hatchbacks, little more than 13½ ft. long in the five-door version, with a slope-nosed front and fastback rear. It had a modest (by American standards) four-cylinder engine of 1.7 litres developing 70 bhp. Yet it was capable of 90 mph and returned around 30 mpg, the sort of performance the American government was seeking to encourage in place of the country's traditional long wheelbased gas-guzzlers.

Ford Escort

The Escort began in 1968 as a low-priced bread-and-butter saloon with 1098 cc, 1.3 litre and 1.6 litre engines, a replacement for the Ford Anglia. It rapidly achieved a distinctive character for by the end of its first year it had won the British rally championship, and in saloon car racing held eight out of nine British circuit records in its class. During the Seventies and Eighties, it developed a range of rally and race-bred competition models including the GT, Twin Cam, RS1600 and Mexico, with engines of up to 2 litres. By the Eighties the fastest Escort was the XR3i, a two-door front-wheel-drive hatchback with a fuel-injected 1.6 litre engine developing 103 bhp. This had a top speed of 116 mph with a 0–60 time of 9.7 seconds.

Morgan 4/4

The peculiar appeal of the Morgan is its traditional appearance, and it is still individually produced by traditional methods. Sheet steel is used on an ash wood frame and each car is road tested before delivery. "A true sports car of traditional appearance", said the Morgan sales literature of 1983, citing the weatherproof hood, fresh-air heater and opening side windows as if written in the Thirties. "Lively, safe and will out-perform all other cars at the price", it claimed, the four-cylinder 1.6 litre engine of 98 bhp giving it a speed of around 105 mph. There has always been a queue of enthusiasts waiting to buy a Morgan.

Dutton Phaeton

Kit cars enjoyed a new popularity in the Eighties as the labour costs in motor manufacturing rose, for the home builder could achieve an unusual car of high performance at a real saving. A traditional looking two-seat sports car with a prominent roll-over bar, inspired by the Lotus Seven and Morgan, and intended to provide cheap, no-nonsense wind-in-the-hair motoring, the Phaeton was based on Ford engines of 1100 cc to 2 litres and Escort components. Some 20 or 30 kits were being sold monthly at around £665 in 1983, and the Sussex company claimed to be Europe's largest suppliers of kits.

Eagle SS

The Eagle had more contemporary styling, including distinctive gull-wing doors, but it also came as a kit from Sussex (Dutton and Eagle had originally shared the same premises). It typified the versatility of kits in the Eighties for the Eagle could be based on a Volkswagen or a Cortina, and kits could be bought at around £1,500 or just below £1,000, depending how much the do-it-yourselfer wanted to do himself. The kits were supplied with instructions and diagrams and could be assembled, according to the makers, in about 120 hours' work.

Tyrrell-Ford F1

Surrey timber merchant Ken Tyrrell began his own racing team in 1960 and moved into Formula One in 1968, but his 1971 car was the first to be both designed and built by his team. It housed the Ford-Cosworth DFV 3 litre V8 engine then used by most racing teams, in a body designed by Derek Gardner, and fitted with the aerofoil wing low over the tail introduced in the late Sixties. Bouncy little Scottish driver Jackie Stewart won six Grands Prix in it during 1971 and became world champion with nearly twice as many points as his nearest rival, Sweden's Ronnie Peterson, who drove a March-Ford. The picture shows Stewart on his way to victory in the British Grand Prix, which he won at an average of 130.48 mph.

Renault RE40

In 1983, for the first time, the world championship was won by the driver of a turbocharged car. All the way through the season it had seemed as though the champion would be France's Alain Prost driving for Renault, who pionered turbocharging in Formula One, but in the last round he was pipped by two points by Brazil's Nelson Piquet in a turbocharged Brabham. Renault concluded that the turbocharger units of their 3 litre V6 engine had been too small. Incidentally, when Prost won the British Grand Prix he lapped Silverstone more than five seconds faster than Stewart had done in 1971.

Ford Capri Turbo

The Capri was, in some ways, Europe's answer to America's Ford Mustang — not a sports car, but a sporty-looking coupé. It was built in both Britain and Germany from 1969 with a variety of engines from a four-cylinder of 1.3 litres giving a speed of about 95 mph to a V6 of 3 litres capable of powering the car to nearly 120 mph. In 1982 a turbocharged V6 engine of 2.8 litres was introduced to the range, which gave a speed of 140 mph and a 0–60 mph time of six seconds on the road; in rally and racing trim (as shown) the Capri was considerably more potent. Ford had sold a million Capris by 1973 when it became a three-door hatchback, and it went on selling well, its styling apparently ageless.

Datsun 280ZX

The first cars Japan exported were regarded in the West as good value for money as they offered as standard many fitments manufacturers elsewhere listed as optional extras, but performance cars they were not — until the arrival at the start of the Seventies of the six-cylinder Datsun 240Z, a 127 mph 'muscle car' in the parlance of America where most were sold. It won the tough East African Safari Rally in 1973. A year later it was superseded by the 260Z with the engine enlarged from 2.4 litres to 2.6, and in 1981 came the Datsun 280ZX with a fuel-injected 2.8 litre engine, a sporty coupé with removable glass panels forming most of the roof over the front seats.

Nissan Cherry Europe

Most of the first Japanese cars had conventional layouts with front-mounted engines driving the rear wheels, but soon there were cars in all layouts and the Nissan Cherry Europe of 1983 was a front-wheel-drive three-door hatchback. The word 'Europe' in the name was because it was assembled in Italy from parts shipped from Japan, Italy being one of many countries in which Japanese cars were built by this time. The high-performance model, the GTi, had a 1.5 litre flat-four engine and a speed of 112 mph, with an acceleration time from 0 to 60 of 10 seconds. It had a five-speed gearbox, a boot-mounted spoiler, twin fog lamps, aluminium alloy wheels and a thick-rimmed sporty steering wheel.

Colt Starion
Turbo

A top performer among Japanese exports of 1983 was this two-door, 2 + 2 sports coupé, its turbocharged four-cylinder 2 litre engine taking it from 0 to 60 mph in just 7.5 seconds, and onwards to around 135 mph. An opening rear window and rear seats that folded flat catered for excess baggage and other features included energy-absorbing bumpers integral with the body at the front, an air scoop on the bonnet, pop-up headlamps, and seat belts mounted in the doors.

Lotus Esprit Turbo

It was an Esprit that was seen driven under-water in the 1977 James Bond film *The Spy Who Loved Me*. That was, of course, a one-off modified version of the car, which had originally been launched as a limited edition model but becoming the replacement for the Europa from 1976. It was a mid-engined two-seater with an aerodynamic wedge-shaped glass fibre body by Giugiaro. The engine was a four-cylinder of 2.2 litres which, with a Garrett turbocharger (a later addition) and a five-speed gearbox, gave 210 bhp, enabling the car to go from 0 to 60 in 6.1 seconds and on to 145 mph, yet returning 33 mpg at a constant 75 mph.

Triumph TR7

"A front-engined car with mid-engined looks" boasted the makers of this wedge-shaped two-seat coupé of 1976, which bore little resemblance to its predecessors in the TR series of open cars. It had been designed with the American market in mind, hence the emphatic safety bumpers. The four-cylinder 2 litre engine developed 105 bhp and gave a speed of 108 mph, which rose to 114 mph in its later five-speed gearbox form. Then it acquired a Rover 3.8 litre V8 engine and became the TR8, but production ended in 1981. It was the end of a popular range which had started back in 1953.

Mercedes-Benz 450SLC

The name of Mercedes-Benz continued to stand for the finest in engineering, though exciting sports-racers gave way to more sober executive cars of traditional layout, a front-mounted engine driving the rear wheels. However, they were still powerful cars, this exclusive coupé introduced during the Seventies being capable of 130 mph with a 4.5 litre engine, or 135 mph with a 5 litre fuel-injected V8, as in the model pictured. Engine, boot lid, bonnet lid and wheel rims were all made of light alloy, saving 100 kilograms in weight; and it was fitted with front and rear spoilers to improve the aerodynamic properties.

Mercedes-Benz Geländewagen 230GE

The range of four-wheel-drive cross-country vehicles expanded considerably in the Seventies; Mercedes launching this 'land car' in 1979. There was a choice of two wheelbases, three bodies, including three or five doors, and five engines, three petrol and two diesel, of 2.3 litres to 3 litres in size. The picture shows the 2.3 litre petrol-engined long-wheelbase model. Normal drive was to the rear wheels, with the option of engaging front-wheel drive as well. While this was a performance car only in its cross-country role, the 300 GD model with a 3 litre diesel engine could reach 82 mph.

Audi Quattro

Another German firm offered something completely different in four-wheel-drive cars. The Quattro was designed for high performance on the road, the four-wheel-drive being permanently engaged. The idea was not new; the Jensen FF had pioneered it in 1966 but the Quattro was more successful, offering a top speed of around 136 mph and a 0–60 time of seven seconds from its 2.1 litre engine. (There was also the Quattro 80 model, somewhat slower, developing 136 bhp against the Quattro's 200 bhp.) In 1983 it was given anti-lock braking, an electronic display panel and talking check system, and Audi promised that by 1985 every model in its range would be available with four-wheel drive. The Quattro headed a magazine poll as 'top rally car' of 1983.

Porsche Turbo

With its wide tyres and tail spoiler it looked like a racer, but was built for the road and was just about the highest-performance car generally available at the start of the Eighties. It evolved from the 911 coupé of 1964 and had a fuel-injected six-cylinder 3 litre engine fitted with a turbocharger from Porsche's Can-Am racers when it was introduced in 1974. This gave it a top speed of 155 mph, but in 1977 the engine was enlarged to 3.3 litres which brought the top speed up to 160 mph and gave the car astonishing acceleration — from 0 to 60 in little over five seconds. The car had electronic ignition, which was becoming commonplace by this time, and such refinements as an electrically heated exterior mirror and illuminated door and ignition keys.

BMW M1

"Relatively tame" was the description BMW applied to this car with a top speed of 192 mph. But that was only in comparison with another version of it capable of 217 mph! The 1979 car, designed both as a roadgoer and a racer, was preposterously powerful. The 'tame' model, designed to run under Group Four rules for special GT cars, had a fuel-injected six-cylinder 3.5 litre engine giving 470 bhp and could get from 0 to 60 in 4.2 seconds. The faster model, built to run under Group Five rules for sports cars, had a turbocharged six-cylinder unit of 3.2 litres producing an incredible 815 bhp and getting from 0 to 60 mph in under four seconds. Detuned as a roadster it could still exceed 160 mph and get from 0 to 60 in 5.5 seconds.

Ford C100

Reducing drag to improve speed and fuel efficiency was a major concern by the start of the Eighties and this unlovely sports car racer, built by Ford of Germany, was, like many rivals, developed in a wind tunnel to improve its aerodynamics. The result was a drag coefficient of 0.32, low by competition car standards, which it was calculated would help to give it at least one refuelling stop in hand over most rivals in the world endurance championships. Two cars were built initially in Cologne for track testing in 1982 and were powered by British-made Ford DFL 3.9 litre engines.

Ghia Quicksilver

The shape of the future? Perhaps. This was an 'ideas car' built in 1982 by Ghia of Turin and exhibited by Ford in Geneva. It was just on 15 ft. long, a five-seater with a drag co-efficient of only 0.30 resulting from an aerodynamic body and such wind-cheating features as a flush-fitting undertray, retractable headlamps, skirted rear wheels and curved windows which became flush with the body when raised. A V6 Ford engine of 3 litres was located amidships, the short bonnet holding luggage and the spare wheel. It was not intended for production but it shows the lines on which designers were working.

Jaguar XJS

Finally, a look at some of the best of British in recent years. Jaguar continued its name for fast, stylish, value-for-money cars with the XJS, launched in 1975 as the fastest automatic transmission production car in the world. It used the V12 5.3 litre engine from the E-Type in a roomier, two-door, four-seat coupé body with air conditioning, leather upholstery, electric window lifts and central locking, all features that were coming to be expected in luxury cars. It could reach 130 mph in 33 seconds and its top speed was nearly 155 mph. The range of XJS cars was enlarged in the Eighties to include two models with six-cylinder 3.6 litre engines and five-speed manual gearboxes, a coupé and a cabriolet convertible, which was the first open two-seat Jaguar for some years.

Aston Martin Lagonda

Both Aston Martin and Lagonda were at one time owned by the David Brown organisation, but Lagonda cars were discontinued at the end of the Fifties and Brown withdrew from Aston Martin in the Seventies, which resulted in the end of the 'DB' designations. The company was reconstituted with a new board in 1975 and the Lagonda name was revived for this advanced, wedge-shaped luxury saloon packed with gimmicks such as a system which automatically locked the whole car 15 seconds after the key was removed from the ignition, a daunting range of digital instruments, cruise control, pop-up headlamps, air conditioning and electric front window lifts. The V8 engine of 5.3 litres gave a top speed of 143 mph and a 0 to 60 time of 8.8 seconds.

Rolls-Royce Corniche

This was the fastest Rolls of the Seventies, a big convertible capable of 126 mph and reaching 60 mph in 9.7 seconds. Introduced in 1971 and based on the drophead Silver Shadow of the second half of the Sixties, it had a V8 engine of 6.7 litres and automatic transmission. It cost £73,168, which was considerably more than most people paid for their homes, though it was still £10,000 cheaper — and 10 mph faster — than the Camargue limousine, based on the same chassis and power train, which was introduced in 1975.

Bentley Mulsanne Turbo

A painted radiator surround distinguished the turbo model, the standard Mulsanne having a chromed surround. Introduced in 1982 it was possibly the best-finished car in the world, with air conditioning and electric windows fitted as standard. It was quiet and thirsty — giving about 11 mpg overall — but with terrific acceleration for a car 20½ ft. long. The all-aluminium V8 engine of 6.7 litres would take it from 0 to 60 mph in seven seconds and on to 135 mph. The price: £61,744. A similar body (except for the radiator) was used by the Rolls-Royce Silver Spirit, cheapest car in the Rolls range, though it cost about £1,000 more and was 16 mph slower.

Index